PAINTING IN
XVIII CENTURY
VENICE

PHAIDON

I. ANTONIO CANALETTO: *Piazza San Marco*. London, National Gallery

PAINTING IN XVIII CENTURY VENICE

BY MICHAEL LEVEY

PHAIDON PUBLISHERS INC

DISTRIBUTED BY DOUBLEDAY AND COMPANY INC

GARDEN CITY · NEW YORK

© 1959 PHAIDON PRESS LTD
LONDON SW7

PRINTED BY ROBERT MACLEHOSE AND CO · LTD · UNIVERSITY PRESS
GLASGOW · GREAT BRITAIN
COLOUR PLATES: BUCHDRUCKEREI WINTERTHUR AG · SWITZERLAND

FOREWORD

THIS is not a book of biographies, neither is it an inventory of artists. The title conveys, I hope, what I am concerned with here: a city and the painting it produced in one century. The book is to some extent an introduction to a subject about which I am well aware of not knowing enough. Depressed as one inevitably is by the mistakes of the books one has to consult —and no field of art history is so littered by the worthless and the misleading as the Venetian eighteenth century—I am very far from confident that I have made no mistakes of my own. Some particular hostages to fortune are given in the notes at the end, but these need not be read.

In a word, the book is not intended to be exhaustive. And I should like to think that it is not too exhausting.

London, 1959   M.L.

FOR BRIGID
con amore

CONTENTS

INTRODUCTION
page 1

Chapter I
THE HISTORY PAINTERS
page 13

Chapter II
LANDSCAPE PAINTING
page 53

Chapter III
THE VIEW PAINTERS
page 70

Chapter IV
GENRE
page 106

Chapter V
PORTRAIT PAINTING
page 134

Chapter VI
THE PRESIDING GENIUS
GIAMBATTISTA TIEPOLO
page 162

NOTES · BIBLIOGRAPHY · INDEX

Dust and ashes, dead and done with, Venice spent what Venice earned.
The soul, doubtless, is immortal—where a soul can be discerned.

BROWNING

INTRODUCTION

A FEELING existed throughout Italy during the eighteenth century that all was not well, a hint of thunder in the air which did not break into a satisfactory storm until the Risorgimento. The cosmopolitan Venetian Francesco Algarotti, a friend of Tiepolo, Lady Mary Wortley Montagu, and Frederick the Great, puzzled it out. The Italians, he wrote and believed, had conquered the world, illuminated it with science and the arts —yet they were not cutting much of a figure in the present. As explanation the metaphor of sleep came to his aid: Italy was dormant only to wake up soon.

Algarotti died in 1764 and Italy was still sleeping when a very different person, Leopardi, born only just within the eighteenth century, looked round his native land. Leopardi saw the statues and towers of his ancestors, 'Ma la gloria non vedo.' And indeed the Italy of Leopardi might seem in worse case than Algarotti's. Despite stirrings of national consciousness the reality of a unified country seemed far away, while the old organization of powerful independent city states had been smashed by Austria and by Napoleon. Besides, something else had happened in Europe between Algarotti's death and Leopardi's birth: the French Revolution.

Of all the Italian city states Venice could claim to have remained the greatest. None except the Papacy had played such a part in world affairs; in Italy none had challenged the Papacy more strongly, nor did the election of a Venetian Pope in 1758 much soften the Republic's proud defiance. Until the last Venice went through the motions of ruling, even while its kingdom dwindled and its political power declined: an anachronism in eighteenth-century Europe, either splendid and touching or intolerant and ridiculous, depending on whether a poet or a philosopher looked at it. As for the travellers who visited eighteenth-century Venice in such numbers, they mostly gave as much thought to the constitution of Venice as Blackpool's visitors nowadays give to the local council. They merely noticed and exaggerated the insignificant, repeated the comments of the guide-books (themselves usually some years out of date, when not positively inaccurate) and came home to write yet another book of travels.

It was not quite their fault that this so often happened. There was little of beauty in eighteenth-century Venice except outward beauty; prying further only produced unpleasant sights and inconvenient facts. The State had every reason to discourage visitors from arriving at the conclusions of Montesquieu: 'my eyes are very pleased by Venice; my heart and mind are not.' Nor was it likely that the author of the *Esprit des Lois* would find much to approve of there, any more than could Rousseau. But the majority of visitors to Venice were no more intelligent in the eighteenth century than the majority to-day; and this was fortunate for the Republic.

It had become a tourist centre. Its processions and ceremonies served for visitors to gaze at in the intervals of boating and gambling. Its ambassadors were accredited to the courts of Europe, but were ignored. The Republic as an entity lost ground—literally—as the century advanced; it lost contact with its possessions on the mainland. Gradually the State became the city itself, and gradually the actual conditions of life worsened while the carnival still gave an air of spurious gaiety to the moribund organism.

The story of eighteenth-century Venice, a story seldom told, is the story of *The Cherry Orchard*, of the inhabitants also of Shaw's *Heartbreak House*: 'The same nice people, the same utter futility.' Only, at Venice the people were not always very nice and there was at least one exception to futility.

Painting in eighteenth-century Venice thrived in that political lazar house where ordinary people starved and died. It not only thrived, but was virtually reborn as art after nearly a century of active mediocrity. And amid an array of talent it produced a genius in Giambattista Tiepolo, last heir to the Renaissance tradition of Italy. Huizinga has remarked on the suggestive spectacle offered by the decay of over-ripe forms of civilization; Venice is a suggestive enough and understudied spectacle in history, and the late flowering of its artistic stock only increases interest.

The Venetian government was not idle during the eighteenth century. Indeed, as it neared the end of its existence the Republic proliferated with regulations and requirements. An almost insane attention was paid to petty laws for establishing the nobles' dress, details of protocol, the position of benches outside cafés, conditions of work for artisans, import of, and printing of, books. After years of discussion, a Venetian academy was founded for painters, complete with regulations which kept it firmly ruled by the Senate. The State had turned in upon itself; it was everywhere. Spies watched on the Piazza; clerics examined the imported books to see that nothing entered Venice by, among others, Helvétius, Berkeley, Rousseau and Voltaire. The Senate even reduced, without permission from Rome, the number of religious feasts. The Inquisition of Three was a reality; accusations it received were acted upon promptly, and when the painter Northcote arrived in Venice (as late as 1779) it was with a shock that he saw displayed in the Piazza one morning a dead body bearing the legend, 'For treason against the State.' The tragedy of secret anonymous accusations became comedy in the last days of the Republic when finally it was the Inquisitors who were accused—and condemned, no doubt.

Against this sinister and hopeless background, hopeless because it revealed the State's inability to govern by open law, the Republic conducted grand ceremonies and proclaimed feasts: the vulgar and stupid formula of bread and circuses which had already proved its inefficacy with the Roman Emperors. But ceremony and display needed its pageant masters, and the painters whom the Senate did not patronize for pictures might at least make themselves useful by designing carnival pavilions, decorative barges, painting or engraving portraits of aristocratic persons appointed to official positions, or simply might reproduce the more splendid feasts in souvenir pictures. These were really the only ways in which painters could serve the Republic officially; and even portraiture, so popular with governments in other countries, received little state patronage at Venice. The titular ruler of the Republic, the Doge, was usually painted once on election, though seldom again.

But the Venetian ceremonies, with their studious parade of appearances, are perhaps one key to the artistic activity of the city. Venice itself, with its marble-faced palaces that are brick behind, is all appearances and illusions, and the life of the city in the eighteenth century was full of appearances. The Doge, who seemed to rule, was really the Republic's slave—his personal likeness did not even appear on Venetian coins. The nobles who seemed so haughty and grand were often desperately poor; there was a good subject for painting, the Abbé Richard thought, in seeing the subservience of a rich but mere citizen when speaking to a ragged nobleman. And sometimes when the Senate seemed about to strike, it thundered but no bolt fell: 'a parade of appearances', said the lucky Lorenzo da Ponte, who escaped with a reprimand for one of his poems when he had feared imprisonment.

This topical aspect of life could find little direct expression in painting. It is significant that the ragged noble and the prosperous citizen—who would have seemed to Hogarth good material for a conversation piece—were never painted by any of the Venetian genre painters. Satire and keen observation were not in demand. Nor did the State encourage freedom of thought. When Casanova tried to sustain the paradox with Voltaire that nowhere was one more free than at Venice, Voltaire replied accurately enough: 'Oui . . . pourvu qu'on se résigne au rôle de muet.' The view pictures of Canaletto and many others, which are so often thought typical, were chiefly produced for tourists not natives. What was a fundamental need, however, was for pictures a little removed from reality: scenes of mythology, whether classical or religious, and of history. And the decorative qualities of these mattered much more than what they actually illustrated.

Decorative pictures, charming rather than serious, were to the taste of the whole age, but nowhere more than at Venice was there such steady demand and supply. The Republic was retreating before reality, playing Canute to the remorseless tide of facts which lapped against it. Examination of itself only proved what could not be said publicly: the commerce of the city was irreparably damaged by the great number of Mediterranean ports; the State archives, especially those of the Inquisitors, were in confusion; even the book trade was collapsing, not so surprisingly in a city where books were burnt publicly in the Piazza. Nor did the Republic really want to be remedied, fearing that the cure would prove unpleasant. Scipione Maffei drew up a very conservative plan of reform in about 1736; it never reached the Government proper (a Government Kafka would have enjoyed depicting) and remained almost unknown until 1797. From these unpleasant facts there were distractions just as useless as, but considerably more beautiful than, the promulgation of petty laws.

Painting offered one convenient and secure retreat, not so much from the present but from the future. In the secret instructions drawn up in 1786 for the French ambassador to the Republic there occurred the significant remark that for some years past there had reigned at Venice 'une sorte de terreur de l'avenir'. Venice herself perhaps seemed no longer under divine protection; worse, there were rumours that even divine protection was no longer an unassailable concept. It does not seem an illogical step thence to the hasty production of splendid altarpieces and frescoes to decorate new and rebuilt churches, nor to the grand ceremonial portraits which enshrine so floridly those Venetian civil servants whose efforts held together the crumbling fabric for a few more years. And other pictures delighted the eyes with their playful homage to another religion, neither state nor ecclesiastical but classical. Poetry, history, and mythology were all blended to produce a style of picture frankly imaginative; and in that pageant world people were dressed in the costumes of the great days of the Republic, the sixteenth century that Veronese had once incarnated in his work.

All these different types of picture went on being produced at Venice long after they had fallen into disfavour elsewhere. Various reasons, not relevant immediately, had caused them to fall into disfavour; but reasons, like reality, could for long gain no admittance at Venice. When reality came, it destroyed the Republic. And when the reasons finally penetrated they sapped the impetus of painting. Venetian painting expires with the fall of the Republic. A few artists, even one or two great ones, lived long enough to see the day when the Tree of Liberty was set up, in 1797, on that Piazza where the Republic had exposed its dead criminals, burnt modern books and served coffee. But the painters are inactive shadows like Alessandro Longhi or, like the old impoverished Guarana, they are sadly active and begging for a pension. The artistic scene at Venice at that period is lightened only by the arrival of the youthfully talented and self-confident Canova, giving the city the benefit of being the site of his early triumphs.

Connoisseurs and Patrons

VENICE had never had the reputation of being an intellectual city. A book published there in 1744, *L'Idea generale delle scienze*, sounds a solemn and solid tome but actually was sixty-eight pages long; and it may stand as symbol of the learned 'appearance' rather than learned actuality which the city professed. During the eighteenth century when so many books were published to explain painting and painters, Venice produced few apologists for the type of painting most typical of it and few biographers of its artists. Thus Canaletto, Guardi, Pietro Longhi, Tiepolo, among those now famous, were none of them thought worthy of individual biography, for one cause or another. As for the style of unlearned painting practised at Venice—a style which may conveniently if loosely be termed 'rococo'—this was left unsupported by any doctrine of aesthetics, was usually left undefended and, indeed, seems almost to have been left unobserved by Venetian critics of the period. To speak of 'Venetian critics' is to suggest a body of informed opinion. However, no such body existed, or if existing it has left no records of itself. On almost every aspect of painting in eighteenth-century Venice on which it would be desirable to have information Venetian records are at best silent; at worst there are no records.

Only one eighteenth-century person in Europe showed real inclination to compile factual information about living painters at Venice—not only inclination but determination: Jean-Pierre Mariette. For it was not, of course, in Venice that the inclination showed itself. Mariette's efforts were praiseworthy and persistent; but he was growing old and sickly in Paris, still trying to compile his dictionary of artists, and he was easily misled by the inaccuracies, the distortions, and the well-meant vagueness of his Italian correspondents.

To the general neglect of modern Venetian painters by Venetians—neglect, that is, to record anything except occasionally that their pictures were beautiful—must be added the neglect by Europe in general. An extraordinary bifocalism may be observed, for the very foreigners who were ecstatic before Canaletto, and were aware of Guardi, failed to notice Tiepolo; while the Venetians who praised Tiepolo virtually never mention Guardi and cared little for Canaletto. And neither party had anything to say of Pietro Longhi. This is so generally true that any exceptions which may emerge in the following chapters here have little significance.

It is the silence of the Venetians that drives us to the visitors who at least put down something, however trivial, on paper. What they say about eighteenth-century Venetian painting is usually vivid, even if deficient. It would be frightening if the artistic life of eighteenth-century London or Paris had been recorded chiefly in the comments of foreigners, but of course in those places that is not so. The artistic life of Venice, itself so popular with visitors and so dependent on its visitors, is better reflected in travellers' accounts than in native comment. The travellers brought a sharp sense of perspective to what they said; they knew painting other than Italian, which is more than most Venetians did.

Yet they could not help being deplorably ignorant. Modern pictures were only occasionally mentioned in their guide-books; they had no other means of knowing whose pictures they were looking at, and in many cases must have liked a picture but could make no mention of it. Extraordinary gaps appear in their knowledge. The Président de Brosses thus lists a great many modern paintings and painters in Venice, specially for the benefit of a friend; the most striking omission in that list, as in all his letters, is Tiepolo—a painter to whom the French, unlike the English, were by no means indifferent. A painter like Pietro Longhi, most of whose work remained in the private rooms of private palaces, could hardly be known to the ordinary visitor. A portraitist like Rosalba—ready to serve foreign princes and tourists—was bound to become famous with her patrons; Alessandro Longhi, a portraitist never working for foreigners, remained totally unknown.

Even the public pictures at Venice were not so easily seen, physically. Bergeret and Fragonard complain how difficult it was to see pictures in Venetian churches: a complaint that Ruskin was to echo more eloquently, and which is far from irrelevant to-day. And Cochin found himself cautiously peering up at a ceiling and saying that it *appeared* to be by Tiepolo. While the bad condition of canvases, especially old ones, made them hard to see, the light in the churches was, and is, often poor. The virtues of eighteenth-century fresco-painters could hardly be appreciated in a gloomy church; and travellers in general paid little attention to frescoes as opposed to oil paintings. Venice was packed with pictures. The modern painters also had to compete for attention with the great names of Titian and Veronese and, to a lesser extent for the eighteenth-century, Tintoretto. It is not therefore surprising that the minor history painters in eighteenth-century Venice are seldom mentioned by visitors.

Yet, despite everything, there were a number of people living in Venice who were interested in modern painting and who could comment perceptively. Some of them were not connoisseurs or patrons, but merely had some interest in what was happening in the city. Thus a Venetian patrician, Vincenzo da Canal, wrote a life of the great painter of his day, Lazzarini, and also fragments of a treatise on the Fine Arts; somehow, it is part of the city's insouciance that neither was published until long after his death. The patrician diarist, Pietro Gradenigo, kept notes of many artistic events along with notes on other aspects of daily life; his comments run from 1748 to 1774, often disappointingly terse but occasionally interesting and always useful. Pictures unveiled, churches consecrated, artists exhibiting their work in the Piazza or at San Rocco, these are the minor diurnal happenings which he noted and which in many cases would have otherwise been lost to us.

Venice did not produce many diarists; few people wrote memoirs, and the city itself lacked a native contemporary chronicler. Gasparo Gozzi, poet and journalist, attempted to provide a newspaper which should mirror life as *The Spectator* had in England; but the truth is that Venice could only with difficulty support the institution of a newspaper and Gozzi's experiment soon failed. While it lasted Gozzi had

II. GIAMBATTISTA PIAZZETTA: *An Idyll on the Sea-Shore*. Cologne, Wallraf-Richartz Museum

managed to 'cover' the same annual San Rocco exhibitions of pictures, and had expressed his preference for the type of 'reality' in painting which he found in Pietro and Alessandro Longhi.

Gozzi was simply an *amateur*, and an isolated one. For *belles-lettres* neither flourished nor were encouraged at Venice, and there was no society where poets and painters and literary men could meet and talk. The greatest literary personality, Carlo Goldoni, left Venice finally in 1762. Indeed when Baretti arrived in Venice from England in the same year he found that conversation, civilities, morality and literature were utterly unknown there; Baretti had the standards of Dr. Johnson and Mrs. Thrale to apply, and he was a peculiarly critical person, yet the fact that he remained three years at Venice is not a reason for dismissing all he says as exaggeration. And Gozzi himself, reporting in 1765 on the crisis in the book trade, states quite openly that Venice lacked the sort of writers that England, France and Germany possessed.

In fact it was in the earlier years of the century that there had been a group of internationally-minded and receptive connoisseurs at Venice, closely connected with painters both Venetian and foreign. As these people grew old and died, their places were not taken. Contact with Venice as an artistic centre dwindled, as Venice grew politically more isolated and out-of-date. England had been the great market for things Venetian throughout the century, yet by 1789 John Strange writes to his agent Sasso in Venice complaining that there has been a change: old and foreign things were despised, 'modern rubbish' is the fashion. Well before that, however, from the other great market of Paris, Mariette reported the shift in taste which had substituted for Italian art that of the Low Countries. Writing in 1769, he recognizes that his own taste is out of date; people now spend vast sums on Netherlandish work, while an Italian painting or drawing is regarded only 'avec une sorte d'indifférence'.

It had been very different when Mariette was young. At Venice, Rosalba and Sebastiano Ricci were then drawing the attention of Europe to a Venetian renaissance; Venetian painters and decorators were travelling all over Europe and meeting their confrères. The links between London, Paris, and Venice were close. Rosalba was in touch with Crozat and Mariette at Paris; they brought her into contact with Watteau; Sebastiano Ricci paid Watteau the chief compliment Ricci could pay: he copied his drawings. In England Rosalba's brother-in-law Pellegrini was acting as her agent; Anton Maria Zanetti the elder, friend of Rosalba, stayed at Mr. (later Consul) Smith's house in London, visited Hampton Court and made English friends. Francesco Algarotti visited London and Paris. (Consul) Smith settled in Venice. Apart from Smith, all these people kept up correspondence with each other, swapped engravings and gems, drawings, bits of gossip, mutual praise and well-turned compliments. Between Mariette and the elder Zanetti, himself an engraver

B

and a *marchand amateur*, a friendship subsisted for nearly fifty years and was broken only by Zanetti's death.

Zanetti is indeed one of the chief uncreative personalities on the Venetian artistic scene. With his identically named younger cousin, the librarian of the Marciana, he forms a phenomenon which touches most aspects of the period. The cousins collaborated on two volumes of classical antiquities at Venice, a project the elder had first conceived perhaps as early as 1722 but which finally appeared— *Delle Antiche Statue Greche e Romane . . .*—in 1740 and 1743. Neo-classic before his time, the elder Zanetti was yet early writing in praise of Canaletto, acting as agent for Sebastiano Ricci at the court of Turin, and finding no division between his various interests. Later neo-classicists were to use the club of learning to batter the heads of people like Ricci and Tiepolo. Zanetti was learned but far from humourless, and his sharp observation of life is well shown by his amusing caricatures— often mildly ridiculing opera singers of the day. He had a collection of pictures and drawings, chiefly by Venetian fifteenth- and sixteenth-century artists but with one or two 'modern' things such as two pictures by C. W. E. Dietrich and a group of Marco Ricci gouaches: some idea of what it contained is given in the letters of Sasso who acted as agent at Venice for a number of English collectors, as well as Strange, late in the eighteenth century.

More relevant for painting than the elder is the younger Anton Maria Zanetti, who lived long enough to see the rise of every Venetian painter of importance. His *Della Pittura Veneziana*, published in 1771, was an attempt at a history of Venetian painting from earliest times to the latest age. For him, quite rightly, it is Tiepolo who dominates the scene; the less public painters receive much less attention, Pietro Longhi being barely mentioned, Marco Ricci only very briefly, and the Guardi brothers not at all. In part Zanetti is on the defensive, aware that there is a case to be made against the whole Venetian School from Veronese onwards; in a learned age, as the eighteenth century had become, he had to admit, for example, that Veronese had not painted for scholars and that his historical inaccuracies were compensated for by beauties in the actual painting.

Zanetti did not embark on a complete defence of 'rococo' painting; he himself reproved such excesses and frivolity, and in the Europe for which his book was written it would have been nearly impossible to do otherwise. He had planned the book for a long time, and it is perhaps a pity he had not published it earlier. Early in life (in 1733) he had amended and added to Boschini's guide to Venetian art, the *Ricche Minere*. In 1760 he had published *Vecchie pitture a fresco*, which attempted to record frescoes in Venice and which has, among other things, given us some idea of what then remained of the work of Giorgione and Titian on the Fondaco dei Tedeschi. More than connoisseur, he was a historian; that, he says in his preface to the *Della Pittura*, he has tried to be. There is no evidence that he himself collected pictures. He read carefully what others had written about the Venetian School, especially among his foreign contemporaries, and in *Della Pittura Veneziana* he compiled a book which has retained all its original usefulness.

Among those who subscribed to the Zanetti cousins' *Statue* were (Consul) Smith and Francesco Algarotti. In their very different ways these two are the most vivid personalities among patrons at Venice. Joseph Smith had never sought European contacts; his sphere was Venice and his passion the most extensive collection formed privately in the city. Apart from his patronage of contemporaries, he had collected pictures by Rembrandt, Bellini, Mantegna and Vermeer—to name the most interesting; his library too had been carefully assembled and well stocked. It is not odd that he should have sought immortality for himself, his books, and his pictures, by offering them for sale in 1762 to George III, an offer accepted by the King. Even after most of them were sold, his passion for collecting broke out again and he assembled more pictures and *objets*. Above all, his patronage of Canaletto has brought him posthumous fame as it brought him sour criticisms at the time. Horace Walpole, with his accustomed generosity, sneered at Smith as the 'Merchant of Venice', and somehow Smith was supposed to have exploited Canaletto. In fact, whatever their business arrangement, Smith must have encountered in Canaletto the same hard bargainer as other people did.

Whatever shady things there were in Smith's life, they are irrelevant to him as a collector. Friendly and of an age with the elder Zanetti, he patronized chiefly the painters of their own generation, collecting many paintings and drawings by Marco and Sebastiano Ricci, and pastels by Rosalba. He was perhaps too old to appreciate Guardi's view pictures, and seems never to have had much interest in Tiepolo. As well as an array of Zuccarelli's work, he had, unusually for an Englishman, pictures by Pietro Longhi; one of these seems to have been a special commission to Longhi and was a group portrait of John Murray and his family, Smith's brother-in-law and the English Resident at Venice.

Smith, finally appointed Consul, remained throughout his life a collector. And he remained a Venetian by adoption, never apparently returning to England. He is not typical either of Venetian patronage at the time or of English patronage. He was eccentric and is still something of a mystery; nothing survives of his attitude to the individual painters he patronized, nor of his attitude to those he did not.

Altogether more loquacious, ambitious, vain and pretentious, Count Francesco Algarotti made one or two stays in his native city and affected in some instances the art of the day. He yearned, however, for higher things than Venice could offer; like many other homosexuals, he had a mild obsession with royalty, and the courts of London, Dresden, and—most successfully—Berlin underwent his siege. Algarotti's acquaintance was as wide as he could make it; even in death he sought new and important connections, bequeathing a group of drawings and a cameo to the

elder Pitt, whom he had never met. At Venice his reputation was quickly established. When he returned there in 1743, charged with the task of acquiring pictures for Dresden, a contemporary sardonically recorded the fact and recalled that
some years before the comedians of the San Luca Theatre at Venice had intended
to put on a comedy ridiculing him.

Algarotti was the chameleon of the age, changeable, charming, intelligent, eager
to please but anxious not to be deeply committed: either in literature or in love.
Though he died prematurely at Pisa in 1764, aged fifty-two, he had not had too
prosaic a life. He had written on opera, and Russia, and the Incas and architecture,
and the Art of Painting; and most of the European celebrities of the day had had a
visit from him. He was in touch with Mariette, who remembered him with affection. Frederick the Great paid for his tomb. And busy as Algarotti always was, he
had found time, too, to form a collection.

When Newton was the fashion Algarotti had written on Newton. It is part of his
admirable ability to keep up to date that in his advice to young painters he should
already have expressed neo-classic doctrines. They should, for example, study
ancient coins and medals; not only for correctness in drawing *but*, and the 'but' is
the serious neo-classic sequel, so as to be familiar with the appearance of those
personages whom they will later paint. At the same time, Algarotti did not fail to
appreciate the chief offender against this canon at Venice: Tiepolo. It must be
allowed that he was sincere in his friendship for Tiepolo, proud of it and adept at
utilizing it.

Back at Venice in 1743, he quickly extended the original schedule of Old Masters
required by Dresden to include also the modern Venetian masters. Perhaps
this helped to check criticism at the time that he was despoiling Venice of its
treasures. He commissioned work from all the leading Venetian history painters.
He offered to the powerful Minister at Dresden, Count Brühl, painted flattery
planned by himself and executed by Tiepolo: the Fine Arts kneeling in a noble
building with Brühl's palace in the background; the goddess Flora bowling along
in her chariot in a landscape with the Neptune fountain from Brühl's garden. And
no doubt Algarotti thought Tiepolo's pictures greatly improved by the dash of
learned sycophancy which he had contributed. For he must have been well aware
that the greatest Italian painter of the day, one moreover whom Algarotti was to
praise for his immense imagination, was not learned by nature.

Beneath his parade of learning, Algarotti was probably Venetian enough to
appreciate and understand Tiepolo. He himself eventually visited the Villa Bar-
baro at Maser and appreciated there the brilliantly decorative and quite unlearned frescoes by Veronese, while in his writings he deplored Titian's anachron-
isms when dealing with Roman soldiers and found faults in the classical learning of
Rubens (who in fact was probably a better classical scholar than Algarotti). He

recommended cameos and medals as subjects for the young student artist; but he himself enjoyed sketching fantasy Oriental heads and helmeted warriors, copied in some instances out of Tiepolo's *Banquet of Cleopatra*, a picture which remained obstinately a fantasy even after Algarotti had done his best to make it scholarly and Egyptian.

As for his collection of pictures, this was partly formed not on principle but by bad luck. Occasionally in his dealings with foreign and royal patrons Algarotti found he could not sell them some picture which he had already purchased; like many dealers he thereupon put the picture into his own 'collection', whence it could always become available later. But from contemporary painters in Venice he bought, or acquired, pictures which do represent his own taste; he had a good Piazzetta, a Pittoni, an Amigoni, a *Self-Portrait* by Ricci, and the largest group of all was made up of paintings and drawings by Tiepolo. In his collection or in his writings, both quite extensive, he names most of the leading painters of the day, in the rest of Italy as well as Venice; but like the great majority of his contemporaries he says nothing of the Guardi brothers, and—perhaps more significantly— never mentions Pietro Longhi.

Algarotti would not have cared to be thought a purely Venetian phenomenon. In his fashion, he was a European; there were other cosmopolitan Italians of his type, though very few Venetians, and none so showy. Despite his title of Count, actually bestowed by his friend Frederick the Great, Algarotti was of the middle classes, a stratum of society not active as patrons in eighteenth-century Venice. The Church and the aristocracy remained the two great forces behind patronage; they were even to some extent *one* force since the great churchmen were nobles, and a well-bred air of fashionable similarity exists between Venetian religious pictures and secular ones. Both types of picture deal with an elevated world of noble, handsome beings, whether historical or divine: a fairytale world, enchanted, in-bred, courtly, where reality was kept at bay. According to one historian, satires were in fact directed at Venice against religious pictures painted with this profane air in which the Virgin often looked as if she was the goddess Flora; these satires (if they exist) only confirm the extraordinary similarity between the two types of picture.

The Painters

THE majority of painters worked to commission. There was not much corporate sense among them and when finally an Academy was founded at Venice it was in no sense a parallel body to the Académie in France or the Royal Academy in London. Nothing illustrates better the easy carelessness of its affairs than the fact that a year or two after Zuccarelli was elected president the Academy had to admit it had no idea where he was.

After years of discussion the Venetian Academy was formed in 1750. From the first it was hardly more than a teaching college. The government showed little interest in it, and the Academicians showed even less. Not only did it plan no exhibitions, but it strongly objected to being required by the government to exhibit pictures in the Piazza at the Ascension Day carnival; the painters presumably thought this would be of little benefit to themselves, and year after year they complained of the difficulties and expense. The chief long-term benefit of the Venetian Academy has been that each member was required on election to present a reception piece and these form a nucleus of eighteenth-century works in the present-day Accademia gallery at Venice.

Painters wishing to exhibit their work publicly in the city could either show in the Piazza San Marco, on their own initiative, or on the feast day of S. Roch (16th August) at the Scuola di San Rocco. On that day, when the Doge went in solemn procession to hear mass at San Rocco, the painters hung up their work partly perhaps as decoration and partly as self-advertisement. These San Rocco exhibitions are really the nearest form to an organized exhibition that took place in the city, except that there was no organization, there were no catalogues, and hardly any foreign visitors to the city knew of the annual event. And, finally, the references by natives were disappointingly terse. In all these ways the event was typically Venetian; it had the same haphazard air as the Academy's proceedings, but seems to have been quite free from government interference (if indeed the government ever noticed its existence).

Other Italian cities had for long possessed Academies and had arranged exhibitions of one sort or another. Outside Italy, Reynolds and Diderot excelled any critic or connoisseur whom Venice could produce. The attraction and importance of Venice, artistically speaking, lay in something much more vital than any of those things: its painters. It was a foreign visitor to the city, Cochin, who summed up the situation as it seemed to him at the mid-century: 'Venice can still boast of possessing the most skilful painters in all Italy, and such as can rank with the best to be named throughout all Europe.'

Such a statement might seem chauvinism on the lips of a Venetian, or sentimentalism on those of any foreigner except a Frenchman. From its source alone the statement compels our belief, tinged with amazement. But Cochin was honest and correct; and what he said cannot be put better.

I

THE HISTORY PAINTERS

ONE innovation in eighteenth-century Venice (one of the few in that conservative city) was the specialization of certain painters in branches of painting: branches which form the subject of subsequent chapters.

When the century opened, no group of painters occupied a more important position there than the history painters. Indeed, the great majority of painters were history painters, by which term was meant painters of figure subjects derived indifferently from religious or historical or classical sources. Yet the position of the history painter throughout Europe was really being challenged by other categories; and hardly a great history painter but found it convenient to cultivate also the portrait. In England in the early years of the nineteenth century Haydon was going to waste his energies in trying to make history painting a reality. And the status of the history painter dwindled everywhere. Well before the end of the eighteenth century Lessing in his *Laokoon* had rebutted the idea that the painter must take his subjects from poetry; indeed, he specifically named, among poems unsuitable for illustration, Dryden's 'Ode on S. Cecilia's Day'. That poem was one equally specifically chosen years before by Algarotti for illustration by Tiepolo. As for the treatment of historical and literary themes in decorative terms, it has been left unattempted by anyone of genius or talent since Delacroix's death in 1863.

But in the Venice of the early eighteenth century history painters still possessed prestige and patronage. The demand at Venice itself for their work was so constant, and the occupation so dignified, that hardly any painter—whatever his speciality—but could produce a history picture when called upon. Guardi spent the earlier portion of his life exclusively as history painter and was still painting a few altar-pieces long after he had begun to specialize as a view-painter; Pietro Longhi painted some atrociously bad frescoes; and even Canaletto is recorded, rightly or wrongly, as having painted a *Holy Family* for a church at Mestre. In addition, there are pathetic shadowy people caught up by the general demand and barely capable of satisfying even a rural parish priest in frescoing his village church: cousins and brothers and sons of better painters, or simply misguided persons with no talent at all, whose work provides the art historian with unconvincing excuses to reconstruct their mediocre personalities. Such people—the painters not the art historians—decided to be respectable if they could not be creative and they form the murky, mercifully anonymous background against which the brilliant history painters of the age must be seen.

Not only is there a murky background to set off the scintillations of the best history painters, but they emerge from an equally murky past: the shadows of the seventeenth century when Venetian art had reached its nadir. Venice had then attracted painters not by what it was producing but by what it already possessed. Nearly every great European painter of the seventeenth century had visited Venice and had felt the influence of Titian or Tintoretto or Veronese. Minor foreigners came to Venice and occasionally stayed on: to become the best painters in this dead and dreary milieu. Painters like Johann Liss (*ca.* 1595–1629) and Carl Loth (1632–1698), both German by origin, are ornaments of the seventeenth century in Venice whereas at another period or elsewhere they would barely have excited attention. Their Northern ideas found an echo in the Venice of their day and Loth in particular, with his thundery chiaroscuro and his prosaic treatment of classical or religious themes, represents a taste of the period for what is in effect watered-down Rembrandt. His *Mercury and Argus* (fig. 1) with its dramatic contrasts of light and gloom, and rudely rustic old man and god, is typical enough of this work. It provides antithesis to what was to come.

So dreary are the immediate antecedents to the renaissance of the eighteenth century that some historians have dutifully unearthed geniuses from the period to liven it up. And it is sadly true that the practice of painting did go on as busily as ever in seventeenth-century Venice, and the city was probably as full of painters then as afterwards. Some of these painters exercised influence on later and greater men; probably both Loth and Liss were influences upon Piazzetta, but Piazzetta was exceptional. In general, when the eighteenth century came it was a revolt from the ideals, the teaching, and the practice, of the previous age; and what is true of Venice is also largely true of the rest of Europe.

During the early part of the eighteenth century, it was not only in and around Venice that Venetian history painters found employment. Foreign courts and foreign rulers, often with much more money and much grander projects in mind, turned to Venice to find artists trained in decoration; and the artists themselves turned to *nouveau riche* countries like Russia where demand always exceeded supply. Northern Europe, especially, suffered already from *fatigue du Nord* and nostalgia for the South with its long tradition of graceful luxury. The cold, petty courts of Electors and Prince Bishops needed an infusion of that warmth and a delusion of grandeur. Versailles still stood as the epitome of grandeur, and for those who could not build so big in reality it was something to have vast palaces built among the clouds painted on the ceiling of a drawing-room. It is in art, as Freud has pointed out, that there is omnipotence of thought. Man, consumed by his wishes, produces something similar to the gratification of these wishes and by means of artistic illusion this playing calls forth effects 'as if it were something real'.

So the history painters became in their way theatre painters, turning every room

1. JOHANN CARL LOTH: *Mercury and Argus*. London, National Gallery

they decorated into a stage, and life was lived amid a series of enchanted illusions. Just as the suites of rooms opened out one from another, so the walls of a room opened out in painted vistas, while beyond the windows stretched the artful perspective of terraced gardens which in the compass of a few acres would suggest infinity. The furniture too of such rooms was often full of ingenuities of concealed space, *meubles à transformations* where spring catches released panels and drawers, and those *tables volants* which could rise or sink through the floor, effectively seeming to defy by magic the natural laws. Everywhere space was supposed, even where it plentifully existed. But space is not exhilarating until something moves within it and reveals its area: like an aeroplane in the sky or even a single camel in the desert. In the space created by the history painters man moved, or rather, beings moved who resembled man but who, unlike him, triumphed in this element. Gods and goddesses are the natural inhabitants of such a sphere, and so is God himself. The religious decorations have no difficulty in repeating the effects of profane decorations, and subjects like the Ascension and the Assumption can be painted in a spirit almost of envy at those miraculous feats of divine levitation.

Towards such effects the Venetians of the century aspired, and all their pictures, whether painted on canvas or on a wall, are to some extent conceived within these decorative conventions. The style itself offered every possible danger, now empty and rhetorical, now overblown and heavy, at one time too flagrantly insincere, and too melodramatically intense at another. Conjurers with varying degrees of skill, they played throughout the century to increasingly empty houses; only one genius rose and out-soared them all, Giambattista Tiepolo, and even he began to face hostile criticism some years before his death.

Outside Venice the problems raised by decorative painting had already been solved during the seventeenth century. The Baroque style had already envisaged tremendous and stupefying effects which surpass nature and leave her gazing. Venice, itself so unfitted for the solemnities of the Baroque manner (however it is defined), had had no Baroque painters nor truly Baroque architects. The great building of seventeenth-century Venice—the sole great artistic feat of the city in that century—was Longhena's S. Maria della Salute; and it is hardly an exaggeration to say that this church with its air-borne domes and sea-washed steps needed merely to be brushed on to the canvases of Canaletto and Guardi to become rococo.

Rococo before its time, it was suitably decorated by a non-Venetian painter, rococo also before the time, Luca Giordano (1632–1705). He left three altarpieces in the church, of which the *Presentation of the Virgin* (fig. 2) with its elaborate architectural setting and its radiant shafts of light preludes the new style and also provides a welcome piece of grand decoration amid the gloomy darkness of seventeenth-century Venetian art. Despite its grimy appearance to-day, the picture is really painted with startlingly bright cool colours: there is generous use of white and a strong blue juxtaposed to it—very much as Tiepolo was to juxtapose them half a century or so later in the Palazzo Labia frescoes. The commission for these altarpieces was given to Giordano in 1685 and reveals that the visiting artist was preferred for this important work to any native talent available at the time. Giordano's legacy to Venice did not go unperceived, it seems, and a few years later the style of his altarpieces was no longer an isolated phenomenon but, made more graceful and less vigorous, had become a Venetian style.

2. LUCA GIORDANO: *The Presentation of the Virgin*. Venice, S. Maria della Salute

Giordano, Neapolitan by birth but peripatetic by inclination, anticipated the personality of Tiepolo: brilliantly rapid worker, in demand at European courts, improviser of extensive fresco schemes, and finally leaving the impress of his style on a whole group of other men. The tradition of Giordano himself was to be closely followed at Naples, and throughout the eighteenth century there was a specifically Neapolitan school of decorative painting which counterpointed the Venetian.

At Venice, there had once been much greater prototypes than Giordano in decorative painting. There had been, above all, Veronese. His decorative ideals had been partly obscured in the seventeenth century in Venice while something more sombre and prosaic was in fashion. With the coming of fresh attitudes, he was to be rediscovered. In an age demanding frescoes, he as a uniquely great fresco painter was bound to become the master of those practising the technique. Titian had painted only one fresco scheme (and that at Padua); Tintoretto had painted none; but Veronese had left at least a single masterpiece, the frescoes in Villa Barbarigo at Maser, and his followers had frescoed other country villas of the Veneto. In an essay on such frescoes Valéry has summed up their decorative, half-mythological, half-country world as 'a blend of poetry and trickery'; and just this blending was to be the intention behind so much of eighteenth-century Venetian decorative work, both frescoes and oil paintings.

Not only in Italy were there stirrings towards those ideals. All over Europe there were signs that grace and charm and a sort of delicate poetry were to be sought in art, partly in relief from the learned academic aspect of art in the late seventeenth century. Painters had been becoming increasingly learned, without in any way improving their pictures; in reaction painters were to become, with much less difficulty, unlearned again. A new age, priding itself on being civilized, was to make civilized use of art: synthesizing architecture, furniture, painting, to create a setting graceful and inhabitable. At the very end of the seventeenth century, in the autumn of 1699, Louis XIV seems to celebrate and initiate the change. In a note on the re-decorating of a château for his favourite daughter-in-law, the Duchesse de Bourgogne, he stigmatized the subject chosen as 'too serious'; and he concluded his criticisms with a command that seems to have found an echo throughout Europe: 'Il faut de l'enfance répandue partout.'

In Venice particular conditions caused particular results. One of the most striking was the fact that Venice had behind it such a magnificent tradition, in art as in government; perhaps the tradition was rather an albatross hung about the eighteenth century's neck, and it certainly led to a neglect of contemporary painters by many visitors. The English, for example, did not object to the religious pictures of Titian, though they ignored those of Tiepolo. Admittedly this must have been partly the sectarian prejudice from which post-Reformation England has usually suffered, for French critics like Cochin were of course far from neglecting contemporary Venetian history painters. To the mid-eighteenth-century connoisseurs in Europe 'painting' meant History painting, unless otherwise indicated. At Venice when the Academy was founded the majority of foundation members were naturally history painters.

The tradition of Venetian art and life met most opulently and obviously in Veronese's work. Venice herself had been present there more clearly than in the pictures of either Titian or Tintoretto. And there the Republic had seemed at the height of success and pleasure and health: its men magnificent, its women blonde and alluring, and itself Queen of the Sea. Since so much of Venetian eighteenth-century painting was concerned with fantasy as opposed to fact, it is not surprising that Veronese offered the safest fantasy-refuge of all in an age when the Republic was yearly shrinking. Backward glances to the past were more than the habit of painters; but the eighteenth-century painters felt a natural kinship with the High Renaissance rather than with the immediately preceding century. And kinship showed itself in the flattery of imitation. Veronese's influence was everywhere, and it extended beyond painting even to Venetian porcelain of the period on which his compositions were occasionally reproduced.

The flattery of imitation showed itself most patently and importantly in Sebastiano Ricci (1659–1734). Almost everything that happened in Venetian history painting of the century goes back to Ricci. He is a disconcerting phenomenon since he began so much, while yet as an artist remaining insipid and usually uninspired. His very attachment to Veronese leads to comparisons in which he emerges eternally the loser. And the existence of Tiepolo, who learnt so much from him, leads to another comparison in which Ricci is defeated again.

But as early as 1705 Ricci was capable of creating the luminous decorative effect of his ceiling in S. Marziale at Venice: an effect considerably enhanced by recent cleaning. To come on this ceiling unexpectedly is to experience something of the excitement it must have generated when it was first shown. It is full of gaily-coloured airborne figures, as in the roundel of the *Arrival of the Virgin's Statue* (fig. 3), and has something of the pastel effect of fresco although all the decoration is actually on canvas. Ricci at this time had not settled in Venice, but was still wandering about Italy and the rest of Europe. He had not become quite so obsessed with Veronese as he was to be later, and the S. Marziale ceiling is an unusual example of him creating something for himself, though not without hints from Correggio.

In the early years of the century the best opportunities at Venice for decorative schemes were offered by the Church. No century has left less artistic legacy in the Doges' Palace than the eighteenth; during that period the government commissioned virtually nothing. Few nobles were then commissioning decorations for their palaces, and in fact most of the history painters quitted Venice at one time or another allured by better foreign projects. Quite early on, England became the goal of many, chiefly in the hope of getting the commission to paint the interior of St. Paul's. That was not, finally, given to a foreigner, nor to a Roman Catholic, but to Sir James Thornhill, whose monochrome decorations represent the finest tradition of English artistic compromise. But the Venetian decorators were employed by

3. SEBASTIANO RICCI: *The Miraculous Arrival of the Virgin's Statue.* Venice, S. Marziale

intelligent private patrons, as they were also employed privately and publicly in France and Germany and Spain. Without too much paradox it can be claimed that the very greatest decorative schemes of Venetian painters of the period are (or were) anywhere but at Venice.

Outside Venice the painters were often called on to exalt absolute monarchies, dignify petty princes and create a mythology to surround quite ordinary events. Their function was to bolster up, with clouds and *putti* and allegorical personages,

4. SEBASTIANO RICCI: *Madonna and Child with Saints*. Venice, S. Giorgio Maggiore

institutions just on the point of decay and collapse. But their work for the one mythology that still had true believers, religion, was less exhausting; the very people they
painted might be supposed to exist, and the people for whom the pictures were
painted might be supposed to be already convinced. Nevertheless, there was little
alteration in the history painters' style for religious as opposed to secular work.

Ricci, having discovered Veronese, set about utilizing him on every occasion.
His 'grand manner' altarpiece of the *Madonna and Child with Saints* (fig. 4), painted
in 1708 for S. Giorgio Maggiore, is consciously derived from Veronese, and an-
nounces the use to be made in the eighteenth century of the casual *sacra conver-
sazione*, where a group of saints are assembled alone or with a presiding figure,
usually of the Madonna. Such a picture as this was soon famous in guide-books of
the period. Vincenzo da Canal was living through the change of taste that Ricci had
initiated, a change which, in his own words, was substituting grace for force in
painting. Partly he lamented this, although he admitted that the new style had a
compensating prettiness and charm. Ricci's altarpiece he had no difficulty in admiring; it was a most attractive picture, a *vaghissima tavola*. And Cochin, sharp enough
in some of his criticism of the modern Venetians, found it *très beau* some forty years
after it had been painted.

To Venetian painters, Ricci's convenient discovery of a style so literally borrowed
from Veronese was to prove sufficient for nearly seventy years. Ricci's pupils went
on quite happily with the method, toning down the plagiarism and livening up the
actual brushwork; they could think of nothing better to do. Ricci himself is not at
all free of the suspicion of having tried to pass his own work off as by Veronese; at
least one of his pastiches was engraved as by Veronese at the time, presumably with
his knowledge. From the French artist Charles de la Fosse, whom he had deceived
with such a pastiche, he apparently received the snub 'Paint nothing but Paul
Veronese's and no more Ricci's'. And there can be little doubt that Ricci felt a com-
pulsive need to imitate the greater man because he possessed no real style of his
own. A large amount of his work is vitiated by its imitation, as well as by its
repetitiveness. Fond of the colour harmonies of Veronese, he never comes near to
rivalling these, and throughout his pictures Veronese is not just an inspiration but a
source to be exploited mercilessly. It was left for Tiepolo to create caprices in the
style of Veronese.

Nevertheless, Ricci's importance as a forerunner was colossal. He was particularly welcome at Venice in the early years of the century, when he finally settled
there, and he was much patronized. He was assisted in the landscapes of his pictures
by his nephew Marco (discussed here in chapter II) and Marco was in the studio
watching out and promising to send to at least one patron anything Ricci executed
in 'his best style'. Ricci, member of foreign academies and doyen of painters at
Venice, led a very grand life in the city; in private he appears to have passed a good

5. SEBASTIANO RICCI: *The Continence of Scipio.* Parma, University

deal of time consuming cheese, for which he was—as he confessed—a glutton. Born at Belluno, he had trained in Bologna and Rome as well as Venice, and his style was full of judicious borrowings from other men's work before he attached himself to that of Veronese. Already before the end of the seventeenth century he is to be found treating certain themes that occur again and again through the following century, often with very similar treatment to his own.

This constant repetition is yet one more remarkable thing about the Venetian history painters: themes like the 'Continence of Scipio', or 'Apelles painting Campaspe' appealed to a mingled sense of the historical and emotional, as did also especially dramatic and poignant subjects like the arrested sacrifice of a virgin (whether derived from the Bible or from classical literature), plagues averted, and miraculous appearances of gods. And already in Ricci's *Continence of Scipio* (fig. 5) we see the eighteenth-century elements present, though the painting itself is probably of about 1695. The theme of such a work lies beneath the apparent subject; this picture is really concerned with love and war, with passion and duty—ideas closely connected with French classical tragedy, and, more relevantly for eighteenth-century history painters, with the same themes as treated in Italian opera of the period. Painters like Ricci often worked for the theatre, and when he was coming to London, horror was expressed by an Englishman living at Rome that 'Rizzi of Venice [whom] everyone knows to be no more yn a scene painter . . .' was hoping to be commissioned to paint the dome of St. Paul's. The inherent theatricality of religious paintings by Ricci was confused with insincerity, then as quite often now; the style that might be permitted when decorating a villa was not going to prove acceptable in an English cathedral.

In fact the same feelings were at work creating, and being satisfied by, the dramatic *Continence of Scipio* and by the religious drama of some alluring female saint. Amid the panoply of war Ricci's heroine occupies a prominent central position as she meekly awaits her fate, while the handsome and magnanimous hero is about to return her inviolate to her fiancé. This incident, supposed to have taken place after Scipio's victory over New Carthage, had for long been a famous event in his biography. Scipio ranked with Alexander as an example of the merciful conqueror; and perhaps there is even a hint, in the many eighteenth-century treatments of such generosity, of Venice herself hoping to be mercifully treated in her impending defeat by the rest of Europe. Leaving that aside, the theme is still one to arouse a sort of delicious pathos and there is an element also of suspense—for Scipio has not yet exercised his mercy. The heroine here, and the heroine more obviously in other similar subjects, is in that state of uncertainty which, caused by sex, adds to her sexual charm. She is a virgin (according to the best authorities) and the century of Richardson, Choderlos de Laclos, and Goethe, derived peculiar pleasure from such an idea, as its literature alone reveals.

To some extent the reaction in the later eighteenth century against such pictures as this is no doubt a sense that they are ambiguous. Connoisseurs and scholars found them lacking in 'seriousness', and this criticism probably includes the persons of the painting as well as the way it is done. Art should improve and instruct, neo-classic aestheticians believed; the painter should follow 'Nature', not his own imagination. There is no attempt by Ricci to convey the aftermath of a real battle, no proper attempt to dress his characters accurately (the page at the left is not only derived from Veronese but dressed *à la Veronese*), and instead of a dignified classical scene we are given at best a decorative anachronistic pageant with a dubious sentimental basis. Later connoisseurs (and earlier ones) would have felt a lack of sternness, a certain melting charming quality which was not suited to a high Roman subject. When Poussin, for instance, had treated the subject, the central figure of his composition was the fiancé not the heroine; she was relegated to the background while the meeting of the grateful Carthaginian and the generous Roman occupied the foreground. Just as the opera of the eighteenth century used such affecting situations but always tacked on a happy ending, so Ricci only plays with our emotions and with the ideas of 'love' and 'duty'.

This, for us, does not affect the picture as a piece of good decorative painting. Looked at, however, as an inculcation of morality the picture is a failure; it is a failure as a document telling us about ancient Rome; and finally it is not true to life, for the colour is prettier than nature and the drawing is not flawless. The colouring of pictures like Ricci's was especially felt to remove their last chance of passing as serious or sublime; 'in historical painting a gay or gaudy drapery can never have a happy effect,' Burke remarks severely in his *Philosophical Enquiry* on the Sublime and the Beautiful. The unfortunate Ricci was to be specifically accused at the end of the century of being the person who caused the downfall of the whole Venetian School. An honorary member of the Venetian Academy, Niccolò Passeri, wrote a two-volume set of dialogues imagined between the great aesthetician Winckelmann and the neo-classic painter Mengs; in one of their dialogues they decide exactly what is the danger of painters like Ricci: such men, bad enough in themselves, are positive menaces because they have pupils whose taste is thus early corrupted.

This much deplored fact is really one of the best things about Ricci. Among his many pupils, Giovanni Antonio Pellegrini (1675–1741), who has been rather neglected by historians, was not only a better painter but a more graceful and lyrical one. Pellegrini indeed is probably the first of the Venetian history painters to paint decorative scenes as such—pure fantasies without any definite story or subject; and these he painted in England. He was in fact the first of the Venetians to make the journey. With him the influence of the theatre was equally strong and much more successfully utilized. The Earl of Manchester, returning from his second embassy at Venice, brought back Pellegrini and Sebastiano Ricci's nephew Marco in 1708.

6. GIOVANNI ANTONIO PELLEGRINI: *Musicians*. Kimbolton Castle School

Recent scholars have drawn attention to the production of Alessandro Scarlatti's opera *Pyrrhus and Demetrius* at the Haymarket the following year, when the scenery was said to be by 'two Italian painters lately arriv'd from Venice'; these must certainly have been Pellegrini and Marco Ricci.

Vanbrugh was already at work at Lord Manchester's seat, Kimbolton Castle, and his grandiose Italianate conceptions are suitably allied with the decorations Pellegrini painted there. Manchester had intended to find in Venice a suitable painter for such work; a few years before he had been ambassador in Paris but does not appear to have made any effort to find a painter there. And from Venice too must have come the magnificent set of florid gilt chairs once at Kimbolton, presumably acquired by him.

Among Pellegrini's various decorations at Kimbolton, some of those on the staircase best display his gift for enchanting improvisation. These decorations are not fresco but are on canvas set into the wall, yet they have all the spontaneity and lightness of fresco. The *trompe l'œil* effect of the *Musicians* (fig. 6) is a piece of light-hearted theatre; Pellegrini half suggests a balcony and space behind, but more as jest than really to deceive. His figures are not stolen like Ricci's from Veronese, but are dressed up in mock-oriental-cum-sixteenth-century Venetian costumes, themselves witty variations on the Moors and pages who decorate Veronese's pictures. They already announce the eighteenth century's love of the exotic: real

7. GIOVANNI ANTONIO PELLEGRINI: *Rebecca at the Well*. Destroyed, formerly New York, Samuel H. Kress Foundation

Negro boys to serve chocolate or carry torches, and oriental clothes to lounge in and to wear at fancy dress routs. Other decorations continue the new taste, with parrots and monkeys, and the scenes are framed by patterns of ribbons and flowers. The whole canvas here is painted with a speedy, flickering touch that conveys light on a creased silk sleeve, a dog's soft fur, the fringe of a curtain: all with an enviable un-English virtuosity that would have appealed to Gainsborough.

Pellegrini repeated his success at other country houses, notably at Castle Howard (which Vanbrugh was then re-building for Lord Carlisle), and at Sir Andrew Fountaine's Norfolk home, Narford Hall. And Wren is said to have favoured him as the painter for St. Paul's. At Narford his silvery woodland scenes are once more a fresh approach to the problem of decoration: with vaguely but far from exhaustingly classical figures and delicately-leaved trees which crowd into an artistic shade. Tiepolo could not have been more than fifteen when such work was painted and his own early years were to be influenced by artists very different from Pellegrini. Yet Tiepolo is the logical development of Pellegrini's style. Had Pellegrini executed his decorations in the Veneto rather than in the isolation of English private houses, he would have been a potent influence, if not on his immediate contemporaries at least on the rising generation.

After England Pellegrini went off to Düsseldorf where he was employed by the Elector Johann Wilhelm during the years 1713/14. Among other work he produced a series of allegorical canvases celebrating events in the Elector's life which are the most elaborate treatment of German iconography by an Italian painter before Tiepolo's work at Würzburg. The lightness and even gaiety of the large *Allegorical Entry of the Elector* (fig. 8) show again Pellegrini's gift for transforming everything into decorative terms; and here the bright pale draperies and the silvery-white of the horses delight the eye and proclaim that the whole affair need not to be taken too seriously. The picture's tone is almost that of pastel, pale as a portrait by Pellegrini's sister-in-law, Rosalba. A few years after his German stay, he was commissioned to paint a great allegorical ceiling in the Banque de France in Paris (probably in 1720) and this had considerable effect on the evolution of rococo decorative painting in France; but once again it left Venetian art unaffected.

Just as Ricci was to face criticism after his death, so Pellegrini did not escape the censure of, for example, Mariette, who lived long enough to see the rococo drop out of fashion. Pellegrini's virtuoso speed in painting the Banque de France ceiling did not appeal to him at all, and it is true that time began to reveal on the ceiling traces of this haste. This, it seems, was made the excuse for its destruction, which Mariette—despite his lack of sympathy for it—deplored. Mariette had loved the soft and rather vague rococo of Rosalba's portraits, but Pellegrini's extended decorative display struck him as too hasty and confused.

Nor did Pellegrini approach religious subjects in a particularly elevated way, and

8. GIOVANNI ANTONIO PELLEGRINI: *Allegorical Entry of the Elector Johann Wilhelm.* Schleissheim, Schloss

it would have been easy to convict him of treating these with a total lack of high seriousness. The theme of *Rebecca at the Well* was one more of those so often repeated by the eighteenth-century Venetians, and Pellegrini's version (fig. 7) is at once partly idyllic and partly flippant. The subject itself, of Abraham's oldest servant producing jewels for the woman intended as a bride for Isaac, appealed as a romantic episode from the Bible—where it is actually dealt with in a strictly business-like way.

There is even, perhaps, a touch of the theme of the pandar in Pellegrini's conception, and his attractive blonde Rebecca certainly seems to be engaged in bartering herself for the old man's jewelry. The scene is not set in a specific time, or even a specific place; it is part of a new feeling that all such details should be generalized as far as possible—a deliberate reaction against the prosaic and more careful attitude of the seventeenth century. Pellegrini thus provides no more than a pair of his silvery-foliaged trees, a fragment of Renaissance-style fountain, and one superior sheep. In this airy setting a snub-nosed Venetian blonde poses with a hand on a property watering-pot, and with an elegant finger retains a piece of rope that is quite unnecessary, granted the type of fountain shown in the picture. Pellegrini is not really *illustrating* the theme of 'Rebecca at the Well' but playing his own variation upon it while, at the same time, dignifying his concept of youth and amorous old age by giving it a Biblical title. Eighteenth-century Venice did not feel strongly about titles for pictures, and when it was necessary to turn Tiepolo's *Banquet of Cleopatra* into a *Banquet of Nabal* for a book of engravings, it sufficed to suppress the pearl in Cleopatra's hand and place a verse from the Book of Kings under the composition.

One other considerable peripatetic decorative painter was active in the early part of the century, Jacopo Amigoni (1682–1752), who has been claimed as the true initiator of the Venetian rococo style. In point of time, Amigoni must yield his claim to Sebastiano Ricci and in grace of technique he must yield to Pellegrini; yet it remains true that his rather pedestrian manner contains the seeds of French rococo, especially Boucher, and it directly inspired Bavarian rococo painting. The hint of the operatic in his style is rather subdued, but he actually painted scenes from operas in which his friend the *castrato* singer Farinelli had appeared. He was not born at Venice but at Naples, and in some ways is the least Venetian—even by adoption—of those who worked at Venice. Like Pellegrini he was active in England (where his portraits pioneered a welcome rococo style which the native school largely ignored), but before that he had spent ten years in Germany, chiefly working for the Munich Court of the Elector of Bavaria.

And so once again it is outside Venice and Italy that his great secular decorations are to be found: at Schleissheim above all, and at the Elector's summer residence of Nymphenburg, in some English country houses, and finally at Madrid, where he

III. GIOVANNI ANTONIO PELLEGRINI: *Two Heads*.
Detail from *Allegorical Entry of the Elector Johann Wilhelm* (fig. 8). Schleissheim, Schloss

became court painter to Ferdinand VI and where he died. In England he received his most sustained patronage from Mr. Styles, the owner of Moor Park, who happened to quarrel with Thornhill, whom he had begun by employing. But in Spain and Germany Amigoni was caught up in the grand new expansionist building schemes of sovereigns: at Madrid in the Royal Palace, where later Giaquinto, Tiepolo, and Mengs were to work, and at Nymphenburg, where the group of buildings and the gardens were constructed, decorated, and laid out by a huge international team.

At Venice only the State could possibly have initiated schemes like these and the State already possessed sufficient buildings. Ricci had found patronage at the Piedmontese court of Turin, as well as outside Italy; Pellegrini had wandered from Germany to Flanders, back to England again and then to Paris. Amigoni remained abroad for much longer periods and had probably decided to quit Italy finally when he left for Madrid in 1747. The pattern of these painters' wanderings was duplicated by many lesser figures, all of them to some extent prophets without honour in their own country and enjoying abroad rather greater prestige than they deserved. The supply of Venetian history painters far exceeded the demand. Although they were at times employed in other North Italian cities they remained very much more likely to be offered commissions out of Italy than elsewhere in Italy, beyond the Veneto. Florence, Rome, Turin, Bologna, Verona, and Naples especially, all had their own little or great local men, some of them working in really appalling provincial styles. A strong sense of rivalry existed, and the more obscure artists often found partial local biographers who made unwarranted claims for their provincial hero; thus a certain wretched Veronese artist, Lorenzi, found a biographer who claimed that Tiepolo had been unable without his help to draw up the scheme of decoration for the Royal Palace at Madrid, Tiepolo being so illiterate and Lorenzi so learned.

In each city the Church became the steady patron of history painters, constant where secular patrons might be inconstant or non-existent. A painter like Amigoni is therefore represented at Venice by pictures *in situ* still in churches, but not by any secular decorative scheme *in situ*; they were never executed or have not survived. Yet we know that pictures of mythological scenes by Amigoni were certainly popular in eighteenth-century Venice and hung in private houses. These needed no particular architectural setting but simply served as ornament to relieve the damasked walls; a painting like the *Venus and Adonis* (fig. 9), while not remarkably novel, is typical of such pictures intended for private owners. Pietro Longhi's genre scenes (discussed in chapter IV) are valuable for the documentation they provide on Venetian interiors of the period from about 1740 onwards, and in them again and again are shown pictures clearly intended to be by Amigoni. Some can probably be identified, either through Amigoni's existing work, or through engravings of it

D

executed about the same time: further sign of his popularity. The *Venus and Adonis* probably dates from his last stay in Venice, between 1740–47, by which time he was no longer a pioneer of anything, and a fresh generation of younger men had formulated a more truly rococo style. Against the new manner, almost exaggerated in its airy elegancies and light-filled compositions, Amigoni's canvases seem naïve and rather Flemish, and sadly unpoetical. And though Walpole is often unfair and obtuse in his comments on foreign painters, when he speaks of Amigoni's manner as 'a still fainter imitation of that nerveless master Sebastian Ricci' and complains that his figures are 'entirely without expression', it is impossible not to feel that he has put one's objections very well.

The rococo idiom had become general. Not only did it extend beyond painting to all forms of decoration and furniture, but it was more strongly present in these than in painting itself. The real excesses of Venetian rococo are to be found therefore in stucco work, or garden statues, or in some elaborate chandelier of glass flowers; and the picture frames of the period are much more rococo than the canvases they surround. While in painting there is no easily apparent and consistent evolution towards a rococo idiom, this can be neatly traced in the evolution of, for example, chairs: from the stiff grandeur of the late seventeenth-century style to the curving, animated and highly coloured variety of styles which represents the peak of rococo. Not only did the furniture begin to riot in a freedom from all discipline, but its decoration was often entrusted to painters of the period who supplied designs even if they did not ever actually execute such work themselves. Amigoni, among others, is said to have supplied furniture designs. Even the cradles of the mid-century at Venice expressed the longing to be air-borne and to conquer space; from one that has survived there rises a long wire with a *putto* suspended at the top holding a coat-of-arms; and others are equally fashionable, and exotic, with branches and birds suspended in the Chinese style. Where the rococo penetrated deepest in Venetian art was in the production of illustrated books, the plates of which are often more fantastic and bizarre than any picture dared be. And the mania for illustrated books resulted in anthologies for every occasion, private and public, where the plates eventually swamped the exiguous text.

So widespread a taste for the rococo probably had an effect upon painters, rather than was in any way inspired by painting. One great painter in fact stood apart from the whole tendency: Giambattista Piazzetta (1683–1754). He is the grand exception to every generalization about eighteenth-century Venetian art, and his personal example was sufficient to create a school of imitative painters non-conformist like himself but unhappily lacking his talent. Unlike most of his contemporaries he did not pride himself upon his speed of execution; rather, he seems to have prided himself on his slowness, which became almost proverbial. 'He is a snail,' reported Count Tessin, arrived in Venice in 1736 from Sweden, going on to praise in contrast

9. JACOPO AMIGONI: *Venus and Adonis*. Venice, Accademia

10. GIAMBATTISTA PIAZZETTA: *S. James led to Martyrdom*. Venice, S. Stae

Tiepolo, who 'executes a picture while another person has hardly mixed the colours'. The decorative painter learnt speed from fresco work—since the paint must be applied while the plaster is still wet—and carried the same principles of haste into canvases. Piazzetta was in no sense that type of decorative painter. He painted only one fresco-style picture in Venice, the ceiling of the *Glory of S. Dominic* in SS. Giovanni e Paolo, and this is not totally successful. His thundery

11. SEBASTIANO RICCI: *S. Peter Released*. Venice, S. Stae

chiaroscuro effects and his feeling for heavy, rather static, drama are much better
conveyed in subjects composed as pictures. His training under a dull naturalist
painter, Antonio Molinari, and at Bologna under Giuseppe Maria Crespi, must
have confirmed these tendencies and encouraged his abstention from any rococo
movement.

His *S. James led to Martyrdom* (fig. 10), painted for S. Stae at Venice in 1717,

makes the work there of the rest of his contemporaries look very slight and artificial
—except for that of the young Tiepolo, who was then briskly and misguidedly
aping Piazzetta's style. It is true that Piazzetta's drama tends here to melodrama;
but it is significant that he has taken a scene lacking in all supernatural incident, and
what he shows in fact is a vigorous old man dragged along in a contorted and confused way by a brawny, tawny, younger man. In character there seems nothing to
choose between saint and executioner. Whereas the rococo, however defined, is
always aiming to elevate the subject to an exciting operatic movement of grand
gestures and radiant personalities, Piazzetta recalls the uncouth literalness of Loth,
for example, and seems almost to 'debunk' his subject. Sebastiano Ricci's *S. Peter
Released* (fig. 11), from the same S. Stae series, was probably painted a very few
years indeed after Piazzetta's picture there, but has obviously nothing in common
with it; real analogy exists, however, between Piazzetta's picture and Loth's *Mercury and Argus* (fig. 1), which was painted a good twenty years before, at least.

While everybody else in Venice was, under cover of a debt to Veronese, going
forward, Piazzetta was going back. While colour was brightening even garishly the
rococo painters' canvases, Piazzetta was restricting his palette to chestnut red,
black, white, and grey. Working within that deliberately narrow range, his genius
achieved at least one great tonal *coup* in the *SS. Vincent, Hyacinth and Lorenzo
Bertrando* (fig. 12) for the new Dominican church, the Gesuati: an altarpiece which
is probably the greatest picture of its kind set up in Venice in the eighteenth
century. Piazzetta has emerged from the grotesquerie of the *S. James* and is also
untroubled by subject matter; he simply disposes his three saints in a cloudy
nondescript atmosphere and from their juxtaposed habits of black, white, and grey,
he makes more effective contrast than would another painter with a whole rainbow
of colours. Unlike the majority of his contemporaries he aims at tonal effects,
gradations and harmonies of monochrome, and he cuts down the amount of light in
the picture in a manner almost rebuking the superb chromatic brilliance of Tiepolo's
ceiling in the same church, also painted in 1739.

The taste for reproducing the trivia of life which runs in Venice from the history
painters to the view painters, via genre, is absent from Piazzetta. The clothes of his
people have a simplicity that is sculptural; and his concentration on the figure, like
his subdued unified tonality, is sculptural too. Perhaps there really is some genuine
relevance in the fact that his father had been a sculptor or a wood-carver; perhaps
from him Piazzetta inherited that feeling for the monumental that makes him stand
out so boldly and forcefully amid the gentle, coloured mists of most eighteenth-
century Venetian art.

Difference was perhaps one of his claims to the interest of his contemporaries.
For while he remained in Venice, his pictures (when he could get them finished)
were in demand beyond Venice, especially in Germany. In the city his prestige was

12. GIAMBATTISTA PIAZZETTA: *SS. Vincent, Hyacinth and Lorenzo Bertrando.*
Venice, Gesuati

13. GIAMBATTISTA PIAZZETTA: *Rebecca at the Well*. Milan, Brera

such that on the creation of the Academy he was appointed first Director. On his death he, almost alone among Venetian painters of the period, became the subject of a biography, by his devoted friend the printer Albrizzi. Most other painters travelled outside Venice, if not outside Italy; Piazzetta seems to have taken no journeys beyond the city and certainly none to foreign countries. And of all the famous painters of the time at Venice he died the poorest. His last years were spent in teaching rather than working, and on his death his widow had to appeal to the State for assistance as he left her virtually nothing.

What he aimed at in painting can be summed up by his version of *Rebecca at the Well* (fig. 13), forceful enough a contrast with Pellegrini's earlier treatment of the subject. Here there is no attempt at the graces of style, and the scene is treated in what may be described as a bourgeois manner: Rebecca and her companions become peasant girls while Abraham's old servant is a rather dashing cavalier in Caravaggesque costume—and we seem to be witnessing a rustic seduction. This 'genre' treatment is, in one way, more real than Pellegrini's treatment, and it leads into the essays in pure genre subjects which Piazzetta also practised (and which are discussed in chapter IV). The painter has once again by-passed the actual Biblical subject and ignored whatever religious overtones might be supposed to be present

IV. GIAMBATTISTA PIAZZETTA: *Rebecca at the Well*. Detail from fig. 13. Milan, Brera

in it. Not only grace and lightness are absent here, but dignity also. In the hands of a painter like Poussin the subject had been grave and even touching; Rebecca had heard the commission with the attention and pose of the Virgin Annunciate. French eighteenth-century critics coming to Venice found Piazzetta's lack of dignity extraordinary, even while they quite liked his work. Although he returned in some sense to the seventeenth century, it was not to those academic standards in which, for example, a king was kingly and a hero heroic. Of Piazzetta's King Darius Cochin remarked with dismay that he had 'the air of a sailor'. Nor would he have had less cause for dismay had he seen the lowering of social and religious tone which the *Rebecca* shows.

Thus, while one aspect of religious painting in Venice at the time exalts the theme into the superhuman sphere (apotheoses and glories and visions), another aspect is represented by the isolated art of Piazzetta which depresses piety into common humanity. Perhaps both aspects were really ways of dodging the religious issue as such in an age when religion was steadily losing ground. And Piazzetta, though praised, did not find a profound sympathizer.

The year 1754, the date of his death, may conveniently mark the apogee of the rococo at Venice. The early generation of pioneers was dead: both the Ricci, Amigoni, Pellegrini, as well as the few interesting strays like Antonio Balestra (1666–1740), who has been crowded out here but whose work tentatively preluded the eighteenth century well into the actual century. Balestra himself is interesting because his was one of the few voices raised at the time against the rococo: the bright colours used by 'modern' painters and their airy compositions roused him to quite open attack. He would have been horrified at being hailed as a pioneer of that style which was triumphing everywhere as he grew old. But with Piazzetta dead, all the great history painters who remained at Venice felt one dominant, ever-present influence: that of the new head of the Venetian Academy, Giambattista Tiepolo (1697–1770). Wherever they had first trained, with whom, by whom influenced otherwise, they could not fail to be aware of the sole genius among them. Tiepolo's own career deserves a whole chapter and is given it (chapter VI), but he is the behind-scenes master for other men's careers. The Tiepolesque idiom is often tedious and silly when practised by anyone other than the master, but then so are the idioms of Michelangelo or Picasso.

The existence of Tiepolo was perhaps most unfortunate for the reputation—in posterity's eyes—of Giambattista Pittoni (1687–1767). Nature may have intended him as the great rococo painter of the day, and certainly he was famous enough and in demand. Possibly he never recovered from the effects of being taught the rudiments of painting by his mediocre uncle, Francesco; possibly he lacked from the first any real vigour or originality, while possessing enough competence to avoid being interestingly bad. And one of Pittoni's chief faults was an eclecticism remark-

E

able even in an age of borrowing. He equipped himself with the means of saying something and then found he had nothing to say.

Nevertheless, that is partly a judgment after the event. Venetian contemporaries did not see the clear-cut division between Tiepolo and the rest of the history painters, and Pittoni formed part of a grand trinity with Tiepolo and Piazzetta. As Tiepolo had succeeded Piazzetta as head of the Venetian Academy, so Pittoni succeeded Tiepolo. Like them he received commissions from Germany for altarpieces, being much more patronized by the Elector of Cologne, for instance, than was Tiepolo. Count Tessin, however, did not care for his work or think him suitable for the Royal Palace commission at Stockholm. And Cochin had reserves about him and about his 'too beautiful colour' combined with empty compositions: another case of Cochin's sharply accurate judgment.

Francesco Algarotti, back in Venice in 1743 from Dresden, also commissioned work from him for the court there; he himself had in his collection a *bozzetto* by Pittoni for one of these pictures, *Crassus sacking the Temple* (fig. 14), which was a subject Algarotti had chosen. And Algarotti carefully remarks in a letter that when choosing subjects for painters he had tried to find those most appropriate to the painter in question. Pittoni was probably considered rather 'learned' and he presents an architectural setting more elaborate than most contemporary painters would have been capable of thinking up. Certainly in eighteenth-century France elaborate classical subjects often had to be planned between the painter and the Académie des Belles-Lettres. Architectural settings, especially classical ones, were well worth the trouble of delineating, and Madame Geoffrin speaks for her age when she says of a picture Vien had been commissioned to paint, 'Temples always make a fine effect by enriching pictures.' The architecture in Pittoni's painting lends it additional value. The subject also is very noticeably drawn from history rather than mythology; it is a good deal more serious and elevated than the love-and-duty themes which were no doubt more popular with Venetian taste. But it remains a moment of high drama, and offers striking contrast between the looting Roman soldiery and the distraught aged priests: it is still an emotional depiction, a clash of wills, and the despoiling of an ancient civilization by a more modern one.

The picture, even if not particularly successful as a work of art, has at least a more 'engaged' air than most of Pittoni's painting, and also a rather more vigorous warm tonality. Unguided by Algarotti, Pittoni inclined to a dreamy, languid rococo style, sugary colouring and commonplace sentiment: too sweetly pious Madonnas kneeling by cribs, and equally sweet classical goddesses. Pittoni is basically sentimental in his art, the only Venetian of the period who is; perhaps part of the vogue in Germany for him at the time is to be explained by his *kitsch* vein, his combination of the homely and the pretty. The languid manner of his altarpieces is often nearly intolerable; but the freedom of his sketches for them, and his sketches also in their

14. GIAMBATTISTA PITTONI: *Crassus sacking the Temple*. Venice, Accademia

own right, show that he had more 'attack' when not needing to work on a large scale.

Considerably humbler than Pittoni in reputation were the Guardi brothers, whose activity as figure painters has excited so much recent attention—chiefly and ironically because of Francesco Guardi's activity as a view painter. To some extent they do present a problem, though they presented few problems to their contemporaries in Venice who hardly heeded their existence. Painters' lives at Venice were not princely and no eighteenth-century artist there (not even Ricci) enjoyed any of the colossal flattering reputation enjoyed almost contemporaneously by artists like Mengs and Batoni at Rome. And at Rome Piranesi, as well as enjoying fame, enjoyed privileges also: such as that of being exempted from paying the tax due on the paper he used for printing.

Painters like the Guardi took what work they could get, and no doubt were grateful. They were very rarely asked to paint a picture for any building in Venice itself. Almost the only religious work acceptably by them (or by one of them), and *in situ*, is that of the organ case in the obscure church of Angelo Raffaele; and the documents that have survived about this do not even bother to name the painter. The Guardi family, though settled in Venice from early in the eighteenth century, came from further north, from Val di Sole near Trento. Domenico Guardi (1678–1716) lived in Venice and had a studio among a small colony of other Trento families, some of whom were related to the Guardi. And it was for this area above Venice that most of the altarpieces of his sons Gian Antonio (1698–1760) and Francesco (1712–93) were to be painted. Nothing of Domenico's work has survived. It is probable that Gian Antonio and Francesco became a firm, a studio from which work was issued as by 'Guardi' and in which the dominant painter was Gian Antonio, the elder brother. There was also a third brother, Nicolò (1715–86), who apparently practised also as a painter, but no work by him either has survived and he may safely be ignored.

Even between the two elder brothers it is often hard to decide which painted which picture, a difficulty increased by the fact that most of the best Guardi work is unsigned and unmentioned by contemporaries. The pictures are very varied in subject and in quality; there are battle pieces and flower pieces, altarpieces, scenes of mythology, and some genre scenes derived from Pietro Longhi. Venice was full of painters copying compositions from each other, but the Guardi never bothered to invent when they could borrow. Gian Antonio copied, for instance, Pittoni's *Crassus sacking the Temple*, copied a picture by Balestra of *Abraham visited by Angels*, copied from his brother-in-law Tiepolo and copied from seventeenth-century painters such as Feti. More often than not he seems to have borrowed via an engraving (such as in the case of the Balestra, engraved by Rotari). In the hands of the Guardi such compositions underwent a change, becoming fluid, wavering and capricious in de-

15. GIAN ANTONIO GUARDI: *The Death of S. Joseph*. Destroyed, formerly Berlin, Kaiser Friedrich Museum

sign and in actual handling of the paint; the line flickers and the tonality grows silvery and misty. Sometimes one can see that the composition has been borrowed, but the Guardi touch conceals its source.

Whatever the degree of collaboration between the two brothers, it is clear that Gian Antonio, the elder, was the dominant partner. Francesco only begins to emerge as a personality we know after his brother's death; indeed, it was only in that year that he got married. Before 1760 documents do speak of Gian Antonio, and of him alone; after 1760 Francesco begins to be heard of, but chiefly of course as a view painter. Gian Antonio may have been head of the studio, but it may be doubted if he was a particularly gifted painter. The signed altarpiece, the *Death of S. Joseph* (fig. 15), which was at Berlin (but was destroyed during the last war), does not give a very encouraging idea of him; those who see him as the painter of the brilliant organ panels at Angelo Raffaele have to date this picture very early. It is, incidentally, a rare case of his designing an original composition for himself.

The organ at Angelo Raffaele was damaged during a restoration to the church in the 1730's. If it had not been, the Guardi paintings would probably never have been commissioned. A new organ, put in some years later, was gilded and its two side wings, or shutters, were painted. At the end of 1750 there was a proposal to collect funds for the purpose of painting the façade of the organ case. The money was to come from charity, as the church itself was obviously too poor. The scheme was humble, and the decorations are modest. No aristocratic person was involved. Two years later it was reported that charity was not proving very plentiful while the sum needed for the work was high, and it was therefore proposed to scrap the scheme.

Then there is silence. The parapet of the organ to-day is decorated, however, and with pictures by one or other (or, very doubtfully, by both together) of the Guardi. A scene like the *Departure of Tobias* (fig. 16) has all the sparkle associated with Francesco Guardi's late views—and the dog alone seems to be by the hand that was to fill views of Piazza San Marco with such lively rapidly-evoked dogs. The tonality of the picture with its pale hues of blue-green and coral has already something of the sea-washed quality of his lagoon atmosphere: a refraction of light which splinters all surfaces and sets every object vibrating.

There seem to be no eighteenth-century records of this series of small pictures *in situ*. They are not mentioned in the list drawn up in 1773 by the younger Zanetti (then Public Inspector of Pictures at Venice) of works of art at Angelo Raffaele; and this has suggested that they therefore date from after that year, so removing the possibility of Gian Antonio's authorship. It is hard to see why Zanetti did not mention them if they were in the church, unless he took them as merely part of the decoration of the organ case and too insignificant to need comment. If so, there is irony in the fact that he, who had lived long enough to see the complete evolution of

16. FRANCESCO (?) GUARDI: *The Departure of Tobias*. Venice, Angelo Raffaele

the rococo style, did not glance at one of its final manifestations. In the Angelo Raffaele series there is the same extremeness as was appearing in France (possibly at the same time), in the work of Fragonard. The prettiness of them is almost a boudoir prettiness; the last vestiges of seventeenth-century solidity and prosaicism disappear and, beside Piazzetta, Guardi seems as incongruous as a butterfly beside a bull.

If the series really dates from late in the century, this would make admirable sense as the last phase in Venice of that desire for air and light which Ricci had largely initiated. But the progress had never been logical or neat; and the Guardi perhaps adumbrated a final phase long before the calendar and historical neatness required. Yet from such an extreme, a return to order was inevitable. All over Europe the last exaggerated elegancies of the style were to be nipped by the colder and more correct standards of the neo-classic; everything that had been set in such quivering motion froze into marble attitudes, and beauty was sought in repose.

Whatever the date of the Tobias series, Francesco Guardi certainly did not cease painting such figure subjects when he took up view painting after his brother's death in 1760. The recent discovery of an altarpiece of nearly twenty years later was a cheerful event since it revealed as by him a large-scale figure work from which Gian Antonio's hand is utterly excluded. This altarpiece, *SS. Peter and Paul adoring the Trinity* (fig. 17), was painted about 1777, once again for a Trento church, this time at Roncegno. It must be admitted that the picture is not quite as good as one would like, or expect; while it is full of rococo *sfumato* and broken touches of light which seem to derive from Tintoretto, it is obviously incompetent and even clumsy. The painter of this is far from reaching the quality of the Tobias series: either because he had not evolved that far, or because he was a different painter altogether.

But the picture is in the same vein of soft (almost scented) rococo which was the contribution of the Guardi to eighteenth-century Venetian art. It is unfortunate that we have nothing to suggest that this contribution was either welcomed or enjoyed in the city: only a curious silence on the subject of the Guardi and their work. And in some ways their style was not very much bound up with conceptions of illusionism and space, or with the imaginative heroes and heroines of Ricci and Tiepolo who peopled such space. They did not manage to organize their work into perspective schemes, being little concerned with depth and space. Their settings are therefore usually nothing but tinted vapour amid which an occasional frond of foliage or a few spikes of grass stand out in Chinese manner. And the people inhabiting this world are equally a blend of the vaporous and the calligraphic. In fact, theirs is a rococo style which is almost aggressively linear and it is significant that the most pleasing decorative work of theirs to survive—apart from the Tobias series—are drawings. Even their paintings aspire to the condition of drawings; they are at once too improvised and too faint to ornament a ceiling or a wall, and expanded to the large scale of altarpieces they look empty. Part of the charm of the Tobias series is its smallness and intimacy, ornamenting not any architectural feature but in effect a piece of furniture.

Meanwhile, the tradition of Ricci continued more obviously and less interestingly in a whole group of painters who were public personalities, discussed at the time whereas the Guardi were not. Of this group Francesco Fontebasso (1709–69) was one of the most distinguished. Like other lesser men he originated as a pupil of Ricci's but was touched by the influence of Tiepolo; and, like so many of the lesser men too, he established a recognizable style more firmly in drawings than in paintings. His art is slight and is perhaps never so successful as in book illustrations, but he worked as ceiling painter, was summoned to St. Petersburg by Catherine the Great and in a two years' stay speedily executed considerable decorative work for her.

17. FRANCESCO GUARDI: *SS. Peter and Paul adoring the Trinity*. Roncegno, Parish Church

18. FRANCESCO FONTEBASSO: *The Adoration of the Magi*. Mrs. J. Maxwell Macdonald collection

At Venice he clearly stood well in the academic milieu. He was appointed a teacher at the Academy, though he seems to have had trouble in getting himself respected by the students, and finally in 1768 was elected President. A small picture like *The Adoration of the Magi* (fig. 18) shows his usual charming feathery touch which helps to lighten the Ricciesque composition, and shows also the small refinements of manner which are really his sole pretence at style: his round-eyed *putti* and saints so consciously attractive, while the colour is richly pleasing. Fontebasso had no fresh comment to make on his subject, not surprisingly, and he therefore concentrated on being agreeable. His pictures provide yet a further illustration of the fact that what is revolutionary in one generation becomes conservative in another. Ricci had actually been dead thirty-four years when Fontebasso was elected head of the Venetian Academy; Pittoni also was dead; Tiepolo was in Spain. Of the history painters in the city Fontebasso must have seemed a very obvious choice for President. In so far as his work shows any evolution, the late pictures show him returning to Ricci's influence; there is no sign of advance, simply a clinging to that style of his youth which had already reached its climax and was in fact in decline.

19. JACOPO GUARANA: *Apollo and Musicians*. Venice, Ospedaletto

On Fontebasso's death there remained in Venice one talented decorative painter in the pure Tiepolesque tradition: Jacopo Guarana (1720–1808), whose activity as well as life continued into the nineteenth century. Guarana, foundation member of the Venetian Academy, is said to have studied first under Ricci and then to have studied with Tiepolo. Of all Tiepolo's many pupils, Guarana was the one who

20. JACOPO GUARANA: *The Sacred Heart and Saints*. Venice, S. Polo

succeeded best in carrying on the decorative tradition. Unlike the majority of contemporary artists, he was employed in the Doges' Palace (where some of his work survives), as well as in other palaces, and in churches.

But his ability is shown in Venice itself most happily in the simple decoration of the music room at the Ospedaletto, painted about six years after Tiepolo's death. This seldom-visited room is a complete piece of *settecento* decoration, in which every available wall space has been frescoed and ornamented light-heartedly and intimately; only the existence of radiators there discreetly reveals that time has passed. The children of the Ospedaletto were famous for the concerts they gave, and Guarana has taken up the theme of music in a charmingly half-humorous, half-poetic Apollo with female musicians who play at one end of the oval room among painted marble columns (fig. 19). The whole deceptive architectural setting is the work of Agostino Mengozzi-Colonna, son of the architectural painter who had been Tiepolo's constant collaborator in such schemes. Agostino's *trompe l'œil* is in the best tradition of his father, while Guarana has peopled it with those vaguely classical figures, in vaguely period costume, who are not taking themselves too seriously.

Part of Guarana's charm is in this unpretentiousness, and even in irrelevance. The dog on the steps is sufficient to tell us that the fresco is Venetian: it has strayed out of ordinary life, to be teased by the woman at the right who extends a doughnut to it, and is a comic adjunct to Apollo earnestly conducting; and it also aids the illusionism of Mengozzi-Colonna's steps. Since Veronese, at least, there had been a cheerful Venetian tradition of irrelevance, if not irreverence, in depictions of solemn scenes. Like his master Tiepolo, Guarana is not concerned with a serious classical world but with creating a piquant and impressive effect: which indeed he succeeds in doing. And Mengozzi-Colonna is concerned with creating an effect of space by a Palladian-style portico of double columns (almost like a miniature of Adam's portico for Osterley) and nothing but sky beyond. First the room is dignified by simulated architecture, its proportions enhanced by the figures, and then the wall is dissolved into the lilac space of limitless sky. Guarana and Mengozzi-Colonna thus assert, for almost the last time, that pre-occupation of their age with illusionism in decoration; and their frescoes in the Ospedaletto close the cycle initiated by Veronese at Maser two centuries before.

A new century is a mere calendar event in an artist's life, and the coming of the nineteenth century cannot have seemed particularly significant to the old but active Guarana. He had survived the fall of the Republic and lived on, probably without quite realizing it, into a new age. In 1802 nothing can have seemed more out-moded than the rococo style, but in that year Guarana signed and dated his altarpiece of the *Sacred Heart and a Group of Saints* (fig. 20) for the church of S. Polo. There is something almost touching in this last expression of rococo ideals, even though as an artist Guarana had never been, nor was to be here, particularly competent or outstandingly talented. He had known Tiepolo when Tiepolo's name was celebrated in half Europe. And here he pays tribute to that pervasive influence upon him, in a picture that breathes the last sigh of the Venetian *settecento*.

II

LANDSCAPE PAINTING

ALTOGETHER on a lower plane than history painters were the landscape painters. At Venice landscape painters as such were few; landscape could hardly be claimed as an individual category of painting there in the eighteenth century, were it not that one or two painters like Zuccarelli devoted most of their lives to it. Even Zuccarelli, however, painted some religious pictures and a few portraits.

Throughout eighteenth-century Europe the landscape occupied a rather equivocal position, as indeed Nature itself did. The landscape of one's own country so often lacked that romantic appeal which the century was always seeking in art. Addison speaks for his age when he says, 'in the wide fields of Nature, the Sight wanders up and down without Confinement, and is fed with an infinite variety of Images.' But a greater variety of images were to be found abroad: above all, in Italy. And in Italy the landscape had already been delineated by seventeenth-century artists whose very names went on evoking down the following century two very different types of landscape painting: the calm pastoral world of Claude and the stormy dynamic world of Salvator Rosa. These, with Gaspard's, were the names that every traveller muttered as the individual effects of Nature prompted him:

> Whate'er *Lorrain* light-touched with softening Hue,
> Or savage *Rosa* dash'd, or learned *Poussin* drew.

But the ecstasies of foreigners were not likely to be echoed by Italians themselves, least of all by the Venetians in their tree-less, water-bound city. Landscape had played its part in Venetian painting, superbly in the background of many of Bellini's and Titian's pictures and quite interestingly in the engravings of Campagnola. In the eighteenth century landscape still needed to be enlivened by people and objects, enhanced by ruins and tombs and peasants; and at Venice it was best appreciated when it was not too literal. Landscape begins to shade off into the 'caprices' of the view painters: blends of two or three views with some prominent monument, a patch of Venetian lagoon, some people looking at a ruin or digging under the stones. Landscape in these pictures is not quite landscape as it was to be in the pictures of Gainsborough or Constable. One of Constable's patrons was to ask for a landscape from which he could feel the wind blowing; that particular fresh and breezy atmosphere was not at all what the 'caprices' aimed at conveying.

Even at Venice there existed a style of landscape hardly related to the 'caprice' but it did not possess much in common either with Constable. The practitioners of it were not view painters, though like them they were often scene designers for the theatre.

The most versatile and important was conveniently the first, Marco Ricci (1676-1729), nephew of the too famous Sebastiano. Like his uncle, Marco Ricci initiates new tendencies at Venice; his ruin-pieces, his romantic scenes, even his sober seasonal landscapes, had each their influence. And Canaletto, Marieschi and Guardi, view painters all, are in different ways indebted to him. As a phenomenon Marco was later overshadowed by his uncle, with whom he had often collaborated, and there is little explicit reference to him by his contemporaries. As a person he seems to have been quarrelsome but convivial.

He was born at Belluno above Venice, and Zanetti in a brief reference reminds his readers of the picturesque countryside around there and speaks also of Titian's influence on him. Marco's admiration for Titian is in fact recorded in a letter. As for the actual countryside, Marco Ricci is untypical of the later Venetian landscapists in his feeling for the countryside of fact; he gives a sense of having felt and seen what he paints of it. Despite being a talented scene designer, he was quite capable of excluding anything overtly theatrical from his landscapes and presenting instead a vivid scene of the countryside under some special effect of weather or season.

A variety of influences jostle with Titian's to create one at least of his styles. He travelled a certain amount in Italy with Sebastiano Ricci, and is said to have spent a further enforced period outside Venice after having split open a gondolier's head. His travels brought him also to England in the company of Pellegrini, with whom he quarrelled before returning again with Sebastiano Ricci. Capable of producing dynamic landscapes of storm and rocks and torrents, he could not fail to be affected by Salvator Rosa's work in this genre. The romantically violent side of Rosa's talent probably was transmitted to him through the bizarre but repetitious Alessandro Magnasco (1667-1735), a person whose work has sidled into exaggerated repute after a century or so of judicious neglect. Magnasco did not work at Venice, and there had been nothing of this kind at Venice, but the two painters may have met at Milan. Marco Ricci's essays in the manner, of which the *Storm at Sea* (fig. 21) is typical, are therefore something quite new in the city, though not generally novel in Italy.

The picture is at once exciting and incredible: it communicates a sense of terror without danger, which is exactly what the century always sought in such scenes whether painted or actual. Even Dr. Johnson had enough of the romantic beneath his commonsense exterior to grow fond of such effects when in Scotland and to think of viewing from a castle on a promontory—rather as in Ricci's picture—'the terrifick grandeur of the tempestuous ocean'. Ricci's adds the yet further excitement of a noble ship being dashed to pieces; in this guise the human element

21. MARCO RICCI: *Storm at Sea.* Bassano, Museo Civico

remains, and we are not witnessing simply an act of Nature but a battle between natural forces and mankind.

The drama is hectic enough, but hardly convincing. The waves rise impossibly high, the promontory with its castle towers impossibly tall, and the whole picture has a typhoon in a teacup air which is like the opening shot of a rather amateurish film. It is not surprising that this type of marine picture found few successors at Venice. For most painters who came after, the sea had quietened into the mill pond of the Lagoon under clear skies and washed softly against the islands with their remains of ruins. A different and less dynamic aspect of the picturesque was found, and one specifically Venetian.

Equally, the romantic extravagance of pictures like the *Cascade* (fig. 22) was to be softened in the later Venetian landscapists. But the *Cascade* remains an anthology of all that the susceptible traveller hoped to see abroad: a wild landscape lit by a lurid sunset and torrents hurtling down amid jagged rocks. And here the mood of the picture is conveyed by the strangely glowing sky with its evening light and pale purplish cloud; unlike the *Storm*, it is something the painter has seen. Subtle effects of light and shade in evoking the mood of a picture were real contributions to landscape by Ricci which remained neglected except by Guardi. Canaletto lights nearly all his work with a cold clear radiance, while Zuccarelli's gauzy but unwavering light is only one aspect of his monotony.

More closely linked to later work at Venice are Marco Ricci's ruin-pieces and architectural pieces. These are closely allied too to his work as scene-designer. In them he often collaborated with his uncle, and the collaboration is as typical as what was produced. Just as gardens needed to be enlivened by statues and grottoes, and indeed ruins, so the pure landscape picture needed a judicious assortment of interesting objects if anyone was to pay it attention. Gradually the landscape element was edged out more and more, and in the hands of someone like Panini at Rome these pictures are ruin-pieces with the minimum of landscape. Italy was the land of ruins. The prestige exerted by the monuments which remained of the Roman Empire had been something very real, especially at Rome, since the Renaissance. And at Rome ruin-pieces became quite serious and archaeological; even when capriciously distributed in a landscape, each monument was recognizable as itself.

In the North of Italy, the mixture of ruin-piece and landscape was more decoratively and carelessly assembled, and fancy replaced archaeology. Temples of the imagination were set amid feathery trees at the edge of romantic lakes from whose shores blue mountains rose steeply; even the landscape became only vaguely Italian. This type of work was extensively practised at Bologna, where whole rooms of palaces remain with frescoed decoration in the manner. And it was a type of architectural decoration that was popular throughout Europe for the stage. This did not necessarily recommend it to everyone and Girolamo Zanetti (a relative of

22. MARCO RICCI: *The Cascade*. Venice, Accademia

the two Anton Maria Zanetti), seeing the opera *Bajazet* at Venice in 1742, found
the scenery a 'strange agglomeration of Gothic, Greek and Roman architecture'.
But in general such mixtures of period and style were enjoyed for their capricious-
ness and fancy.

The two Ricci's collaboration on the *Tomb of the Duke of Devonshire* (fig. 23) is an example unusually elaborate at Venice. These extraordinary 'Tombs' were a series of twenty-four pictures planned as a venture *ca.* 1720 by the bankrupt impresario Owen McSwiny, who was living in Italy to avoid his creditors. Artists from Bologna and Venice were employed in collaboration upon them, including as well as the Ricci, Canaletto, Pittoni, and Piazzetta. The Ricci at least had practice in collaborating together; even if they could not understand the meaning of the various symbols to be placed on the 'Tombs', as other painters of the series certainly could not, they understood the convention. McSwiny managed to dispose of ten 'Tombs' to the Duke of Richmond for the dining room at Goodwood, and there they served as decoration just as the frescoes on the walls of Bolognese palaces.

At Venice elaborate examples, such as those McSwiny had planned in honour of English Whigs, were obviously not going to be in demand. But some tombs do appear in Canaletto's caprices, and a tomb itself, like a monument, had those associations of the past, melancholy yet pleasant, which are finally expressed for the whole century by Gray's 'Elegy'. In Italy too some churchyard poetry was produced, even a musing on *La Tomba di Shakespeare*. As for tombs in art, it must suffice to say that the Ricci themselves were honoured by having imaginary tombs drawn in their memory by their friend, the architect Juvarra.

The ruin-picture, whatever the actual ruins were, remained more popular than a landscape which was simply a view of ordinary countryside. Yet even insipidity could be a pleasure after too much hectic and 'savage' landscape, and as a change also from the ruins which crowded out trees and mountains and nearly the grass too.

Marco Ricci's own straightforward landscapes are far from insipid, as they are far also from the dynamic. It was probably towards the end of his life that he began his small gouache landscapes on kid skin, a material he seems to have preferred. They are a more private and personal aspect of him than any other work he executed; one group of them belonged to Joseph Smith and passed with his first collection into that of George III. Other groups exist, but it is doubtful if they were widely known at the time or exercised any influence. Some rather similar-style etchings by Marco were published in Venice in 1730, but these are more conventional views than he produced at his best.

Since everything must have a prototype, the gouache scenes may be said to have theirs in Dutch and Flemish landscapes which Marco may have seen when returning with Sebastiano to Venice from England. Possibly the uncle and nephew came home via the Netherlands. Marco's gouaches are a more direct depiction of North Italian landscape than anyone had painted previously; and they remain un-Venetian and untypical of their century in their neat and yet poetic realism.

His *Winter Landscape* (fig. 24) is not a prettification of nature, nor a caprice; nothing suggests the scene designer. Instead, and perhaps for the first time in Italian

V. MARCO AND SEBASTIANO RICCI: *Allegorical Tomb of the Duke of Devonshire.*
Detail from fig. 23. Birmingham, Barber Institute

23. MARCO AND SEBASTIANO RICCI: *Allegorical Tomb of the Duke of Devonshire.*
Birmingham, Barber Institute

landscape, winter reigns quite truthfully: from the bruised sky to the frozen water and the frost-rimed trees. The simple effectiveness of the scene, in which people are a few scattered muffled puppets, riding hurriedly through the snow or gathering twigs, is repeated in other gouaches where autumnal and summer moods are captured. The simplicity is such that the pictures hardly seem novel after the vast parade of nineteenth-century landscape, yet their authenticity and uniqueness remains. The mood of the day, the season, the weather, is what Ricci has seen and felt; and he has set it too in the fertile beautiful landscape round his native city. During his lifetime, in the severe winter of 1708, the Venetian Lagoon froze; at least one naive little picture records the scene on the ice. It is interesting, and perhaps even significant, that Marco does not depict that scene. The topical has no place in his landscape work—though he was quite capable of topical witty comment as we know from his caricatures of opera singers. His gouaches of deep countryside, with winding paths where bullock-drawn carts pass under summer trees or labour through the snow, have an almost Virgilian feeling for the soil: serious, evocative and with some trace of sadness.

Zanetti was right to emphasize him as not Venetian. Venice remained urban, severed from the countryside except as that offered a retreat from the city in summer. Gasparo Gozzi, in a lively letter to his mistress who had withdrawn to her villa, sighs for the song of birds in place of Venetian church bells ringing out eight days on end to celebrate an abbess' feast day. But Gozzi is suitably vague about what sort of birds one hears in the country, and at heart adored the bustle and noise of Venice. Birds were more likely in eighteenth-century ears to have the effect that Tickell's 'Woman of Fashion' complains of in Kensington Gardens:

> Whose ridiculous chirruping ruins the scene,
> Brings the country before me, and gives me the spleen.

A park is one thing, but unordered Nature is another. And in the work of Francesco Zuccarelli (1702–88) Nature is kept well in hand, softened from the asperities of Rosa and Magnasco, and kept safely away from the seasonal effects of Marco Ricci. No doubt Zuccarelli, born in Florence but active largely at Venice and in England, felt the influence of Ricci. When he had finished, however, not much trace of the influence remained; he had, in his fashion, created his own style of landscape, with skies forever blue, trees forever green, and the whole scene appearing bathed in sweetened pinkish mist.

So considerable was Zuccarelli's reputation that it is almost impossible not to wish to redress the balance savagely before his pictures. The English particularly were great admirers, and they have since proved his harshest critics. At the time he was preferred to Richard Wilson, and as Wilson is now being worshipped idolatrously the mechanism has operated in the reverse direction. Wilson was himself on

24. MARCO RICCI: *Winter Landscape. Windsor Castle. Reproduced by gracious permission of H.M. The Queen*

familiar terms with Zuccarelli, whom he met in Venice in 1751, and is early recorded as receiving 'strong impressions of colour and effect' from Zuccarelli's landscapes. Probably it was really under Zuccarelli's influence that he took up landscape painting himself, and their friendly relationship is a fact.

In the days before Wilson was a great English genius—that is, when he was alive —he was by no means too grand to think highly of Zuccarelli and he probably also knew incidentally Marco Ricci's landscapes in Consul Smith's collection. Zuccarelli is, Wilson writes home from Venice in 1751, 'a famous painter of this place'. Perhaps Smith, who was kind to the obscure Wilson, introduced the two painters. Smith employed Zuccarelli on some elaborate classical and religious landscapes, and also on some work in collaboration with Antonio Visentini (1688–1782), the architect and engraver. Once again landscape is diluted and improved (sic) by architectural additions: not ruins this time, but English Palladian buildings, the designs of which were sent out to Smith. Thus Burlington House appears in an Italian landscape (fig. 25), without looking quite incongruous. The picture is, rather, a witty blend of two worlds, a caprice of a type growing more and more popular at Venice in these years; the two painters have signed and dated the picture 1746.

Zuccarelli's part here is very humble. The landscape he preferred, and constantly painted, is well shown in the *Italian View* (fig. 26), probably of nowhere in particular. It is just a generalized and charming Italy: imagined as a country with picturesque but well-behaved peasants, delightful weather and pretty rural scenery —not totally therefore a misrepresentation. And at the same time, such pictures are part of the longing for a peaceful refuge: a blending of the pastoral with the classical (itself never far away in Italy). Had Zuccarelli been able to add invention to his gift for composing an attractive pastoral, he might have fared better. Instead, his long life was devoted to reproducing the same effects as here with increasing insipidity and flagging powers. Like Corot, he fell into being a manufacturer of the article that had become popular: varying picture after picture only by minor changes in the peasantry or, less felicitously, decorating it with a supposedly historical subject.

He toyed with religious and classical figures in the landscape and once with the witches' scene from *Macbeth*: they are none of them solemn nor playful; at best they are irrelevant, at worst just silly. His version of *Hercules slaying Nessus* (fig. 27), probably in Zuccarelli's own London sale of 1762, is a rather more overtly romantic landscape than usual and rather better organized. But the comic figure of the child Hercules, a cupid with bow and arrow, is presumably a prettification of the classical story by Zuccarelli, who has got himself into difficulties with an adult Deianira. Instead of Hercules' bride, she appears to be his mother. In this instance the figures are ridiculous to the point of irritation, but the landscape with its vista of water and its castle bosomed among trees has an air of verse if not poetry; it hovers on the borders of enchantment, like the work of some minor eighteenth-century

25. FRANCESCO ZUCCARELLI and ANTONIO VISENTINI: *Burlington House in an Imaginary Setting.* Windsor Castle.
Reproduced by gracious permission of H.M. The Queen

26. FRANCESCO ZUCCARELLI: *An Italian Landscape*. Uppark, Sir H. Meade-Fetherstonhaugh

27. FRANCESCO ZUCCARELLI: *Hercules slaying Nessus*. Glasgow University, Hunterian Collection

poet, and shows that Zuccarelli does not always deserve the sneers of modern English critics.

He had Italian patrons, among them Algarotti who sent off his work to Dresden. And he was praised by Italians: Baretti, indeed, calling him 'mio Zuccarelli', associates him with Ariosto (with whom Diderot was to compare Boucher). Yet, like so many Venetians, he felt the need to travel and again, like them, he chose England. No other Italian painter had such a success in eighteenth-century London as Zuccarelli. He spent on and off some fifteen or so years in England, exhibited at the Free Society, the Society of Artists, and at the Royal Academy of which he was a founder-member. When, after Algarotti's death, the heirs wanted his bequest to Chatham to be taken to England Zuccarelli was chosen to execute the commission, and perhaps was ultimately received by Chatham, who entrusted him with a letter of thanks for Algarotti's brother. In England, Zuccarelli's pictures had considerable success; they remain in hundreds of country houses, those 'beautiful landscapes' which 'must ever please', as Henry Angelo wrote of them.

Certainly Zuccarelli provided a charming enough impression of a country many of his patrons did not know. And a landscape by him was intended merely as decoration, set into a wall or above a fireplace, not as depiction of an actual view at a particular season. Just like 'wings' of scenery, trees flank the composition and a river or a road gently leads the eye towards the pale hills of the distance, past picturesque pines and peasants, into a soft blue infinity. No clouds darken the view, no rain or snow falls, the trees are never bare; such reality would break the spell he is attempting to weave. Arcady had gone through many literary and artistic metamorphoses from its original bleak reality as a district of Greece; and Zuccarelli's depictions of gentle countryside are perhaps the last evocation of it as a deliberately golden-age place. 'A kind of fairy land' Steele says that pastoral poetry should present; it is to the same realm that Zuccarelli attempts to transport us. On the walls of a modern gallery his spell looks very fabricated and flimsy—like Victorian pantomime scenery exposed to daylight; but in a room of the period even the sugary tonality of his pictures plays its decorative part.

Henry Angelo had known Zuccarelli in London and copied his work as a boy. He vividly if inaccurately evokes an incurably penniless painter who was always needing a loan, and loyally speaks up for those pictures which were already passing out of fashion. Carey in his *Thoughts* of 1808 had said 'No artist gave so many charms to the lovely serenity of a rural scene as Zuccarelli.' That was said to a world where Constable had already exhibited at the Royal Academy and where *Lyrical Ballads* had been published, and re-published. By the time the Redgraves were writing on British Art and Artists (in 1866) the tone of denigration was established: 'his rurality rather that of the stage or novel' . . . 'mawkish and pretty insipidity' . . . and then we read of Wilson's striking merits. It was not because Zuccarelli is feeble

VI. GIUSEPPE ZAIS: *A River Scene*. Detail from fig. 29. London, National Gallery

28. GIUSEPPE ZAIS: *A Country Scene*. Venice, Gallerie

that he was condemned, but because he was artificial, and the sturdy morality of the Redgraves, which stresses the 'stage or novel' in puritan tones, would have condemned Tiepolo too if given a chance. Victorian distrust of the Continent has begun.

While Zuccarelli received praise and has gone on receiving attention, even if abusive attention, a much more lonely figure practised landscape painting contemporaneously at Venice: the shadowy Giuseppe Zais (1709–84). Little is known of him and he has remained unknown, largely because his work continues to pass through the sale rooms as by Zuccarelli. Zais's handling is much more vigorous than

29. GIUSEPPE ZAIS: *A River Scene*. London, National Gallery

that of the more famous man who no doubt influenced him; it has something of the 'dash' of Marco Ricci, itself inherited from Rosa via Magnasco. While not afraid of being pretty, Zais's pictures are much more firmly constructed and painted than Zuccarelli's. In some way or other, perhaps via engravings, he must have seen French *fêtes champêtres* and a picture like the *Country Scene* (fig. 28) is partly a homage to Watteau.

Whereas Zuccarelli's people are usually intended to be indigenous to the scene, watering their cattle or posing archly with their flocks, Zais often shows people out for the day enjoying the country. The landscape is evoked solidly and with much less trickery than Zuccarelli used; it is more 'real', though that word is otiose. There is, combined with feeling for the landscape, a French elegance for instance in the figures fishing in the *River Scene* (fig. 29): smartly dressed aristocrats having some fun, who are much more tolerable than the rouged peasants with whom Zuccarelli would have sweetened the scene.

Zais remained totally unknown to the English apparently, and his name never appears in eighteenth- or nineteenth-century sale catalogues. Yet some of his pictures entered the country perhaps as by Zuccarelli (remaining so attributed), for they are not uncommon. But Zais is a mere postscript to a theme which was never fully worked out at Venice. One or two other landscapists existed, among whom Antonio Diziani (1737–*ca.* 97) may be mentioned for completeness' sake. Diziani's bucolic scenes probably did not attract much attention, and it is interesting to find that the Adam brothers owned two of them in 1773, said to have been acquired 'during their long residence abroad'. But it was not in Venice that the landscape of the eighteenth century was created. Rosalba, for instance, is recorded as being highly scornful of Zuccarelli for practising as a landscape painter. The whole category of landscape was not really popular in Italy. Goethe, arriving in Rome late in the century, was amazed at the low estimate of it there. At Rome landscape had merged into the ruin-piece. At Venice landscape was merged with a much more prolific and lively category of painting: the view-picture.

III

THE VIEW PAINTERS

IN Alessandro Longhi's *Compendio* of the lives of important contemporary Venetian painters, a book of portraits with brief eulogistic biographies, no view painters or landscape painters are mentioned. Both categories are pointedly excluded by the title adjective of 'historical' painters. The *Compendio* was published in 1762, when Canaletto was a famous figure not only in Venice but throughout most of Northern Europe. Alessandro Longhi must have been perfectly aware of Canaletto's existence but like many other academically-minded people in Venice he chose to ignore it, as he chose to ignore the existence of Zuccarelli.

The view painters were in some ways yet more humble than the landscapists. Whereas Venetian interiors of the period may well show a Zuccarelli on the wall, they never show a view of the city itself. And the view painters had every cause to be grateful to the tourists, especially the English tourists, who filled Venice. It was tourist demand which called into existence the supply of picture-souvenirs which could be carried back to the North, shown to admiring untravelled friends, and which brought Southern light and warmth into that cold world. There might even exist a sort of therapeutic value in delineations of Venice, and when the valetudinarian Mr. Woodhouse in *Emma* needs to be entertained, Jane Austen has Mr. Knightley produce engravings of 'some views of St. Mark's place, Venice,' which help to while away the morning.

The eighteenth century had perfected the idea of the 'Grand Tour'. It was particularly an English idea and equally specific was its devotion to Italy. 'A man who has not been in Italy', said Johnson (who had not) 'is always conscious of an inferiority.' And the visitors in Venice, eager to be portrayed by Rosalba, were probably eager to bring back further proof of their superiority with a painted view of Venice. Venetians did not want, or need, view pictures. And so the view painters received few commissions from their fellow-citizens; their fellow-painters despised them, and most of them even now remain in oblivion—only the famous names of Canaletto and Guardi being generally known. They had little place in the discussion of art in their own period and none in the period which followed. Canaletto was lucky to get a mention at all in the mid-nineteenth century—even an unfavourable one by Ruskin. Guardi was barely known and seldom mentioned.

But they are among the most important, as they are among the most typical aspects of art in eighteenth-century Venice. Canaletto and Guardi between them have created a concept of Venice which influences those who have not seen it—and those who have. There has never been a city so extensively the subject of such sustained representation; but perhaps that can quickly be explained by adding that no other city has deserved to be. The view painters, besides, are a marvellous tribute to the eighteenth century's rational *use* of art; their pictures have a definite purpose, a purpose the English did not find in the contemporary history painters whom they therefore ignored. Nothing had yet been said about 'tame delineation of a given spot', and the record of 'a given spot' had all the impartial value of an eye-witness record. Enthusiasm was required less than accuracy.

Nor did Venice need any enhancing of the picturesque. It presented, as it still presents, the traveller with an eternal surprise. This was the lure of Italy, in general, and though the sober qualities of the eighteenth-century mind are so often emphasized the age actually loved a good surprise, appreciated fantasy and enjoyed incongruity; it was civilized enough to be the first century which could truly savour and indulge these emotions. 'One finds something more particular in the face of the country (Italy), and more astonishing in the works of nature,' Addison remarked, 'than can be met with in any other part of Europe.'

That ability to astonish was crystallized by Venice, beginning with the enchanting infraction of nature's law whereby it rises from the water; it was a city of the imagination to console those who without it would have had no illusions; it was a *pays lointain* which fortunately turned out not to be too far away. Not only tourists felt its permanent attraction. A native like Goldoni, by no means uncritical of his city and its citizens, looked back to it, the city he would never see again, as an old man in Paris: 'Venise est une ville si extraordinaire qu'il n'est pas possible de s'en former une juste idée sans l'avoir vue. . . . Chaque fois que je l'ai revue, après de longues absences c'étoit une nouvelle surprize pour moi.'

As well as a surprise, Venice offered entertainment with its theatres, cafés, gambling houses, brothels. Its prostitutes were famous and the general air of licence and amorality excited even the sluggish hearts of the English. It was the civilized world's concept of a city, although it had not the glamour of antiquity which took travellers on to Rome. What it lacked in classical ruins it made up in carnival, the delightful air of being for ever *en fête* deceiving many visitors into thinking it an ideal city.

The view painters catered for the eyes alone; they represented, and they did not need to comment. What Goya, for example, would have made of the corrupt but fascinating spectacle is an intriguing question; but the Venetian republic would have dealt with Goya long before his satire grew savage. From the fact of the city's declining power the view painters turned tactfully away; more, they concealed that decline under the splendour their pictures derived from the great pageants so often represented. The pictures became then both views and pageant scenes recalling those of Carpaccio. The annual feasts which the Doge attended at various churches became popular subjects, and each of these was part of Venetian history, a traditional spectacle which age had consecrated and time had made meaningless. Like a simulacrum, the Doge revolved through the pre-ordained circle of pompous empty activity. Painted by Canaletto, such moments as the *Wedding of the Sea*, most splendid of all Venetian festivals, must have made his countrymen proud again; the crowd agog on the Piazzetta that he shows us, a seething mass through which the ducal procession had to push its way to reach the golden, many-oared barge of the *bucintoro*, forgot politics and poverty in the excitement of the day. And in the *bucintoro* the Doge was enshrined as the gilded symbol of the Most Serene Republic —like the Host in a monstrance was Goethe's apt comparison.

With Canaletto and still more with Guardi, the ordinary man sinks his significance until he becomes a mere blob on the horizon, an articulated puppet to enliven the scene:

> His knowledge measured to his state and place;
> His time a moment, and a point his space.

Certainly these figures seem part of the gaiety of the view pictures; and part of the attraction for the English was to gaze at these variegated Venetian throngs. Dr. Moore, one of the more sober travellers, cannot help evoking the crowd '. . . in St. Mark's Place, such a mixed multitude of Jews, Turks, and Christians; lawyers, knaves, and pickpockets; mountebanks, old women, and physicians . . .'. However arbitrarily Canaletto grew to treat this assortment, he did not ever omit them, and in his early paintings he hit off the Jews and the Turks, the raffishness of the loungers and beggars, the pride of a passing senator; and, as the eighteenth century enjoyed its life as mirrored on the stage in topical comedy, it enjoyed these reminders of man amid the topography of Venice.

The view picture was a microcosm. It was basically a product of observation, almost a scientific one since it was often observed through the *camera ottica*, a sort of camera obscura in which mirrors reflected the scene outside. In his dark box, as he peered towards it, the view painter saw his scene compose—rather too steeply in perspective, admittedly, but this could easily be corrected. Canaletto occasionally, and Guardi more often, did not bother to correct the distortion and it can be seen in some telescoped line of buildings, or in a sprawling distant feature which was beyond the *camera ottica's* range of true focus. But in the *camera ottica* the world was mirrored while the viewer watched, himself withdrawn. Life became a peepshow, and the painter himself was no more part of what he saw than somebody looking through a keyhole is part of what he sees.

The Venetians themselves had not failed earlier to peep at their city once or twice. Early depictions, however, had been mere background in a few rare pictures, apart from the series of religious festivals painted by Gentile Bellini and Carpaccio;

and even in that unique example the city itself is subordinated to the religious-civic scene. In fact, Venice was still the active centre of an empire, too absorbed to consider its appearance a subject for painting and not yet a show-place for the tourist. Early in the sixteenth century a few painters do occasionally brush a vague romantic sketch of the Campanile and the Piazzetta, seen from the lagoon, into the far background of a picture: mere reference points to Venice, and by no means views, as in Giorgione's *Madonna* (at Oxford) or Sebastiano del Piombo's *Death of Adonis* (at Florence).

These isolated examples—symbols of Venice as they are—are very different from the careful townscapes of Northern painters. Early Netherlandish pictures are often as topical and as urban as Villon. While Italian art again and again lifts its subjects outside time, Northern artists more usually emphasize the moment of actuality, a room cluttered with everyday objects, a window beyond giving upon an almost unnaturally clear landscape or townscape—as if embalmed in a glass paperweight. This interest in immediacy was to be the impetus behind Venetian view painting. The first painters of the city for its own sake were in fact Northern artists, with their uncomplicated ability for painting what their eye fell upon.

The activity begins in the seventeenth century, at a time when native Venetian painting falters and almost peters out. Just as native talent was replaced among figure painters by foreigners like Liss and Loth, so it was foreigners with equally barbarous names who painted the first tame view. We hear of Corrado Filgher, of Monsù Cussin, Monsù Giron, and so on. Among the less obscure are Joseph Heintz, from Germany, and Richter, from Sweden. Heintz seems to have reached Venice by 1625; a contemporary described him in 1660 as *'l più capricioso*, and the adjective will serve for the lively doll-like figures who cram his pictures. Already it was Venetian festivals which fascinated such painters, and a scene like that of the Patriarch's procession to S. Pietro in Castello (then the Cathedral of Venice) gives a good idea of Heintz's talent (fig. 30). Richter, who did not die until 1745 and is then recorded as eighty years old, is altogether duller; his entry in the register of deaths does not even mention him as a painter, and perhaps he had ceased well before then to struggle on in his unsuitable career. But at the time some people—even painters —could refer to Richter's *genio* for view pictures; Antonio Balestra went so far in 1717 when obtaining small pictures from him.

The first spurts of view painting activity were probably inspired by some sort of demand, Heintz's perhaps by the demand of those involved in the ceremonies he painted. Such patronage was later to utilize both Carlevaris and Canaletto. A superior foreign painter who visited Venice, probably from Rome where he was already settled, was Gaspar van Wittel (1653–1736), whose name was euphonized italianately into Vanvitelli. We know that he was in Venice certainly by 1697, for a view of the city (now in the Prado at Madrid) is dated that year. His pictures of

30. JOSEPH HEINTZ: *The Procession of the Patriarch.* Venice, Museo Correr

Venice are a wonderful tribute to Northern sobriety and commonsense; they make nothing of the city in their cool competence, but they seem to have left some mark upon the first native painter of views, Luca Carlevaris, a Venetian by adoption. Carlevaris (1663–1730) was born at Udine, the son of an architect of sorts, and he seems to have inherited a talent for mathematics. When late in life he came to have his portrait painted (by the well-known portraitist Bartolomeo Nazari) it was with the dignified item of dividers—not paintbrush—in his hand. Nevertheless, it was probably as painter that he was most widely known, a gentleman painter: *Pictor Venetus et Mathematicae cultor egregius*, was inscribed under the engraving executed after his portrait.

In England Carlevaris was probably hardly known during his lifetime. A good deal later in the century his name begins to appear in London sale catalogues. One of the earliest mentions is at the sale of part of a famous Venetian collection of the time, that of Marshal Schulenburg, sold in London in 1775. Schulenburg, last of the condottieri, defender of the Venetian territory of Corfù against the Turks in 1716, settled in Venice and commissioned many pictures from contemporary painters; no doubt his four pictures by Carlevaris were obtained directly from the painter. An earlier reference occurs in a description published in 1761 of Foot's Cray Place, home of the collector Bouchier Cleeve; there are mentioned views by 'Carlevarin' (sic). We know that the English Resident at Venice, John Strange, also sent home pictures by Carlevaris. In Strange's own sale of 1789 there was an essay by him on Italian art, and notes to the pictures. His reference to Carlevaris is probably the first explanatory one in English and it explains also the infrequency of Carlevaris' name in the sale catalogues of the period. 'The first of any note,' Strange says, 'who painted views of Venice; though his pictures are scarce.'

Carlevaris' view pictures, unexciting as they are, are certainly the first we have about which we can make any definite statements; that alone would endear them to art historians. He was not exclusively a view painter, and his career probably opened with caprice scenes of harbours, ruin-pieces and so on—that type of work which goes back to Salvator Rosa and which has its roots in seventeenth-century Rome. His view paintings are something more original, for while he may have been influenced in a general way by Vanvitelli the results are much more interesting than anything Vanvitelli produced. Carlevaris gives us the first really conscious expression of painting Venice to emphasize the importance and the grandeur of Venice. Not the first to take Venetian festivals as his subject, his scenes are often those of Venice internationally engaged: the reception of a foreign ambassador or a regatta in honour of a foreign king. Such grand occasions were recorded in a picture, itself then engraved and so disseminated through and beyond Venice. When Carlevaris produced a book of etched views of the city (issued in 1703), he expressly announced on the title page that the etchings were to make known abroad the splendours of

31. LUCA CARLEVARIS: *The Procession of the Earl of Manchester*. Birmingham, City Art Gallery

the Venetian republic. Visiting grandees often carried home the picture Carlevaris had painted of the scene in which they took part; while it served them as memento, it served also as advertisement for Venice.

With the turn of the century, at the very time Carlevaris published his *Vedute*, Venice needed advertisement of her splendours. The past was needed to bolster up the present. The war of the Spanish succession which broke out in 1700 threatened the neutrality of Venice; she was wooed by both France and Spain, until both countries tired of her evasions and ignored her neutrality. That act by which the Republic suffered French capture of Desenzano and Austrian occupation of the Veneto, was perhaps the first public declaration that Venice had ceased to be a European power. It had once been called the new Noah's ark where liberty was preserved amid a Barbarian deluge. Early in the eighteenth century Italy stopped looking to Venice for a lead; its hope was in Savoy, which did not fail the country when the Risorgimento came.

In a twilight period of humiliations, however politely disguised they might be, Carlevaris was proclaiming Venetian pomp in its ceremonies and pride in its buildings. He himself was patronized by the aristocracy in a way that later view painters were not to enjoy; in their palaces he was probably tutor of mathematics and perspective; he was friendly with the rich and distinguished Zenobio family, one of whose members stood godfather to his son. It seems certain that foreign patrons on their visit to Venice knew Carlevaris was the painter to commemorate the scene of their arrival. When the Earl of Manchester came on his anti-French embassy in 1707, Carlevaris painted the scene (fig. 31), and the Earl took it back with him to Kimbolton. Nothing could be more splendid than this scene; in reality the embassy was a failure, Venice evasive, and the Earl successful only in bringing back to England this picture and some others, as well as Pellegrini and Marco Ricci. The Earl's secretary, Mr. Cole, later published a description of the embassy for which, as for all such occasions, the Venetian protocol was lengthy and elaborate. Significance was muffled in display; policy became an excuse for pageantry. 'The whole Town is in Mask for two days,' Mr. Cole writes of the Venetian custom, 'and there is Musick all night in the Ambassador's House.'

When the Imperial ambassador, Count Colloredo, came on his visit to Venice in 1727 Carlevaris was again available; again the picture returned with the ambassador and is now at Dresden. Carlevaris carefully records the decoration of the ambassadorial gondola, and this in turn had been the work of a decorative painter, a certain Paolo Ovio, who had designed for it a complicated allegory of Peace between Spain and Power. Carlevaris' picture was engraved and itself became almost a piece of Venetian protocol: in later similar scenes Canaletto, for example, always uses the composition Carlevaris had devised. And the same is true of Carlevaris' composition for regatta pictures. He, it seems, fixed the composition always afterwards observed when he painted the regatta given in 1709 by Venice in honour of Frederick of Denmark (who took home a version of the view). That design too was engraved and thus easily available for copying.

An amusing reference to his activity as painter of ambassadorial arrivals is made by the keen nineteenth-century searcher in Venetian archives, Rawdon Brown, who was for long resident in Venice. Brown has noted on his copy of the record of Alvise Pisani's embassy to England in 1707 that the Pisani family then still possessed a painting of Pisani landing at the Tower of London, and he thought this might be by Carlevaris. Unfortunately, this picture seems to have disappeared. If it really were by Carlevaris, it can hardly have been painted in England—since we know he was that year in Venice to paint the Earl of Manchester's arrival—and a Venetian's version of the Tower of London might be worth seeing. In any case, it is interesting that Pisani's embassy to Queen Anne was painted as a record for the ambassador himself—another example of Venetian pride in recording Venetian events. Rawdon

Brown also records that the Pisani family had two other pictures of their ancestors' embassies, both by Carlevaris.

These scenes, though a speciality of the painter's, were only part of his view painting activity. The ordinary busy life of the Piazza San Marco and the Piazzetta —everyday Venice—he has recorded in pictures which have rather more vivacity than his pageant scenes. He was actually capable of very great freedom, in occasional sketches like that now at Birmingham (fig. 32) which probably were studies for himself for use in paintings rather than paintings in their own right. Just as Constable's sketches now seem to us preferable to his finished pictures, so the lively observation of Carlevaris in sketches such as the Birmingham one are preferable to his rather cool completed views. What certainly was a private sketch-book of studies of people for insertion in his pictures is now in the Victoria and Albert Museum; here a lively economical line vividly evokes traders and gossips, Turks and seamen, anticipating in rapid handling the figures of Guardi.

It is odd that with such talent Carlevaris did not achieve better results in his etchings; but probably the Victoria and Albert sketch-book is considerably later than the etched *Vedute* of 1703. The architecture in these—and they are chiefly of buildings—is very feebly conveyed, while there is a monotony about the views which they certainly do not possess in reality. But at the same time the etchings are much more dramatic in their tonality than the pale Flemish tones of Carlevaris' paintings. In place of the steady blue skies of those, these skies are sometimes the scene of baroque dramas of clashing shadow and light darkly reflected in the water

32. LUCA CARLEVARIS: *Boats and Figures*. Birmingham, City Art Gallery

33. LUCA CARLEVARIS: *Rio de' Mendicanti*. Etching. London, British Museum

of the canals. Carlevaris shows in them how much in fact he still belongs to the
tenebrist tradition of seventeenth-century Venetian art, a tradition which in figure
painting is chiefly continued into the eighteenth century by Piazzetta. As Piazzetta
may be contrasted with Tiepolo, so the thundery skies of Carlevaris' etchings are
replaced by the placid skies of Canaletto's etchings and the pastel skies of Guardi's
paintings. In an etching like that of the *Rio de' Mendicanti* (fig. 33), where long rays
of setting sun bar the dark sky, Carlevaris catches transitory effects of cloud that
recall Tintoretto, and the otherwise static scene is given a momentary vivacity. It
is probably because the book of etchings was intended to be a useful work of topography rather than art that he did not attempt such exciting effects more often—
which is a pity.

   Although Carlevaris was the prototype for a number of painters who followed,
he was rather an unacknowledged prototype. Such fame as he may have possessed
was to be totally eclipsed by the fame of Canaletto and, despite some foreign patronage, he was really a private Venetian phenomenon. Carlevaris suffered in fame not
only through the rise during his lifetime of Canaletto but through the comparative
rarity of his paintings. Probably he did not live by his work as painter, though it
does not seem clear how he acquired the tolerable sums that he was able to be-
queath to his son and daughters. He seems to have written no mathematical
works, despite that claim under his engraved portrait of being *Mathematicae cultor
egregius,* and our sole piece of evidence to justify this intellectual claim is the fact that

he is shown there holding a pair of dividers. It is probably not very wrong to see Carlevaris as the amateur, talented but by no means exclusively a painter, still less exclusively a view painter.

The gossipy abbé Gian Antonio Moschini, who wrote about Venetian *settecento* literary life early in the nineteenth century, told a story that Carlevaris' death in 1730 was occasioned by apoplexy at Canaletto's success. Canaletto had been successfully practising view painting for some ten years when Carlevaris died, so the apoplexy was not sudden; more interestingly, Moschini thought, or said he thought, that Canaletto was Carlevaris' pupil, and there seems a vague tradition—but no evidence—of this. For Moschini of course it made a better story and art history is full of legends of artists' fury at their pupils' success, though actual apoplectic death is rare. If Carlevaris did teach Canaletto, the evolution of view painting is neatly linked, for Guardi was hailed early in his view painting career as a 'good scholar' of Canaletto. And these three figures span by their activity ninety-three years of the eighteenth century.

From the first Giovanni Antonio Canaletto (1697–1768) was a professional, one of a family of professionals. His approach to view painting must certainly have been influenced by his early training in stage design, upon which he was collaborating with his father Bernardo and his brother Cristoforo by the time he was nineteen. Although no actual designs have survived we know the names of certain plays for which Bernardo and his sons are recorded as having executed the scenery; and the type of scenery can be gauged well enough. The chief exponents of theatrical *décor* at the time were the Bibiena family, whose complicated architectural perspectives provided the setting for every type of play. One of their favourite devices was the *Scena all'angolo*, whereby the stage setting was constructed at an angle, which gave the spectator a more lively and interesting vista down the pillars and porticoes and balustrades which represented the inevitable location of most plays: a palace interior. The same methods could in any case equally serve to show an outdoor scene, usually a palace garden, where trees and shrubs and statues were arranged in an ingenious perspective. In both cases the audience were treated to a grand panorama before which the actors were dwarfed, and in fact the actors were essential only for the impression of grandeur—just as somebody standing outside St. Peter's is essential to convey the height of its façade.

This sense of 'theatre' Canaletto was to bring to view painting. However, he was not yet a view painter. The staging of plays at the time, and not only in Venice, was an extraordinary business of collaboration rather resembling the mounting of a ballet to-day. The demands of the playwright, of the actors, of the designer, of the manager, and usually—since so many plays were accompanied by music—of the composer, had each to be adjusted, and the project proceeded in a very *ad hoc* manner during the first rehearsals. The resultant quarrels had various results:

actors withdrew to Dresden, playwrights sulked, leading ladies had hysterics. As for Canaletto, he quarrelled with a playwright and consequently, in words reported by Zanetti and probably his own, 'he solemnly excommunicated the theatre.' That was in 1719 and it seems likely that he left Venice at this point for a visit to Rome.

Whether or not he paid attention to the Roman painters of the period, he certainly must have made a number of drawings of Roman scenes, chiefly ruins in the Forum which were a stock subject for any visiting artist. The next year he was back in Venice and is listed for the first time in the artists' guild records. Seven years later he had achieved such a position that a contemporary records that he has 'more work than he can do'. Thence onwards for forty years Canaletto remained busily at work.

Quite early he was associated with Joseph Smith and also with the ex-bankrupt McSwiny. Canaletto was included with other artists working on those extraordinary 'Tombs', two of which were by the Ricci. Canaletto's share in them seems to have been restricted to some figures on some of the Tombs themselves, and his collaboration would hardly be supposed at all were it not recorded in engravings after the compositions. Much more importantly, he produced for Smith over a considerable period of years a wide range of views and caprices, most of them acquired by George III and now in the Royal Collection at Windsor.

'His excellence lyes,' McSwiny wrote acutely in a letter to England, 'in painting things which fall immediately under his eye.' In these early days it was by no means the Venice of Piazza San Marco which always fell under Canaletto's eye. He did not yet work for the tourist market, but rather for private patrons—like Stefano Conti of Lucca, who commissioned two views in 1725 and a further pair in 1726. These show the extraordinarily vivid freshness of Canaletto's eye when he was still young; they are full of an exciting if unsteady tonality as in the *View of the Carità* (fig. 34), which recalls the thundery effects of Carlevaris' etchings and is far more atmospheric than any of Carlevaris' paintings. A little later, probably, Canaletto went further: he was now total master of his powers of realism and he produced '*The Stone Mason's Yard*' (fig. 35) in the National Gallery, unique in his work for its genre qualities, and certainly his masterpiece. Again the view includes the church of S. Maria della Carità, but seen across the untidy area of the 'Stone Mason's Yard'. The view is not of a famous sight; it is rather an intimate behind-scenes view of a Venice seldom seen by the tourist. There is an almost Flemish sense of realism in, for example, the child who has tumbled over and is urinating while its mother gesticulates dramatically. The men hammering the blocks of stone, especially the kneeling man in the foreground, and the broken column with a pair of calipers resting against it, are painted with a serious and almost touching attention anticipating Chardin. And the Venice rising about this 'yard'—actually the campo S. Vidal, the church adjoining which was then being rebuilt—is the weathered shabby

34. ANTONIO CANALETTO: *View of the Carità*. Montreal, Estate of the late Elwood B. Hosmer

city of fact, with peeling walls whose colouring gives the picture a sense of being rain-washed, as does the sky from which the smoky clouds are gradually clearing.

With that painting finished, Canaletto's potentiality to be a great painter was declared and virtually promised. In the first pictures painted for Joseph Smith, mood and intention are nearly the same, but the powerful air of intimacy has gone. And soon Canaletto's great promise had gone too. Out of his large atmospheric early pictures of the city, peopled by real people, he evolved the later small, neatly-lit and neatly-observed views decorated by amusing but mechanical puppet figures—competent souvenirs of Venice for an age before that of picture postcards.

That evolution does not sound very exciting, and Canaletto's progress into mechanical reproduction probably began to bore even him after some years. The years of his first fame are probably the time when he began to assemble some pupils and co-workers in his studio; for vast as was his own output, he can hardly be responsible for all the Canalettesque views we have, even after imitations and frank pastiches have been discarded. No doubt the studio helpers were useful in preparing pictures even when they did not really paint them, and examination of Canalettos of the late thirties and early forties indicates attempts at mass production. Many of the scenes would already be recorded by an original sketch made on the spot by Canaletto and often worked up more elaborately in a further drawing

35. ANTONIO CANALETTO: *'The Stone Mason's Yard.'* London, National Gallery

done by him in the studio. From this second drawing the paintings could be prepared. The practice seems to have been to paint in the sky, and even sometimes the clouds, across the whole upper area of the picture; presumably the buildings were then drawn in over this and certainly their outlines were incised into the sky paint so as to provide guidance for the actual painting of them. Traces of incision are visible along roofs and cornices, semi-circular lines marking arches and domes, and though these are also present in paintings entirely by Canaletto, equally they are preparations which assistants could easily and usefully make for the final brush of the master. In fact many Canalettos show fluctuations in quality within the one picture: now the figures are more clumsy than his, now authentic Canaletto figures enliven a dully-painted architectural scene.

While Canaletto and his assistants worked busily away, the topography of Venice was changing; a campanile fell, a further storey was added to a building, but the master-drawing in the studio remained the model and many paintings issued were in minor ways topographically out of date. At times Canaletto was scrupulously exact. He would paint in perfect detail the reigning Doge's coat-of-arms on the *bucintoro*, in an area smaller than a baby's finger-nail; at other times he painted, for instance, the interior of San Marco and showed it as it had been thirty years before. Partly the immense detail of his pictures is deceptive, intentionally so, in giving us the impression of being eye-witnesses, and Canaletto invests with up-to-date vividness some ducal procession or some Venetian feast that he himself has not witnessed for years.

In the years up to his English visit in 1746, while he was chiefly working for English tourists, he kept also that Venetian by adoption, Joseph Smith, as his patron. Quite what were the business relations of the two men we still do not know. The eighteenth-century English verdict on Smith was that he first bought up Canaletto and then sold his pictures to tourists. No doubt Smith somehow benefited financially from his patronage of Canaletto, but at the same time he clearly liked and collected Canaletto's pictures for himself. In 1735 was issued a volume of Canaletto views in Smith's possession engraved by Antonio Visentini, himself a painter of architectural scenes; in later years expanded editions of this followed, showing the range of views which Smith possessed. Smith collected the work of other painters, chiefly Venetian contemporaries, drawings by them and even caricatures, but Canaletto remained the painter he most extensively patronized. For Smith Canaletto produced a few *capricci*, views of Venice where famous landmarks are piquantly jumbled together to make a capricious non-realistic scene: so the bronze horses of S. Marco are found on pedestals along the Piazzetta, or the Redentore is transported to an island in the lagoon. These were paintings to be appreciated more by the resident or native than by the tourist: variations as they were upon themes which were familiar only to the former.

The intention behind them was sophisticated, just as was that behind the Palladian *capricci* of Zuccarelli and Visentini. Canaletto was really too prosaic to catch the potential enchantment of the idea—that was left for Guardi—and his imagination creaked only too audibly in constructing such things. But the work was a little more dignified than pure view painting, and on such work Algarotti was to employ him at a later date. Algarotti, with his ever-ebullient ideas, did not fail to have an idea about the *capriccio*; in his view it made the best of the two worlds of reality and the ideal: it united 'nature and art'. It was this synthesis which dignified the *capriccio*, making it a part of the eighteenth century's campaign to reconcile what it considered two opposites. Nature, in fact, needed to be sieved through the fine mesh of art; the connoisseur who was not a tourist could only tolerate a Venetian view which was more than a view. In Algarotti's case, he himself chose the buildings to be juxtaposed and so became more than a patron who merely pays: the pictures he commissioned were painted by Canaletto but the ideas were Algarotti's.

The instance was rare, if not unique, in Canaletto's career. Before that he had sought a respite from Venetian views, while continuing to enjoy English patronage, by a visit to England. Armed no doubt with letters of introduction from Smith, he arrived in 1746. By general account the visit was a disappointment to the painter and to his potential patrons; the quality of his work seemed to have deteriorated and soon the rumour arose that he was not 'the veritable Canaletti of Venice' at all but an impostor. And in fact it was a step of doubtful logic for Canaletto to come to England. The English had enjoyed his paintings of, for them, an exotic scene; Canaletto's style by itself hardly lent interest to London views, despite his obvious fascination with the Thames—poor Northern substitute for the Grand Canal. There were possible jobs in painting country houses, a task other foreign artists, such as Wyck, had earlier been set by aristocratic patrons. Had he been a little more generally talented perhaps he would have been set to paint the aristocracy's horses and their dogs. As it was, he visited and recorded Warwick Castle, King's College, Cambridge, Eton and Windsor, in neat, rather old-maidish views, often displaying his incomprehension of English architectural styles; it was only when he was safely back in Venice some ten years later, that he could utilize pieces of English Gothic in *capricci*.

Originally he was the painter of a city, and in England it was London which best brought out his gifts, fitfully but at times with reminiscences of his real painterly self. Broad bold grasp of a street scene, the *View of Whitehall* (fig. 36) shows how instinctively he responded, even as late as about 1751/2, to an urban view. Topography enlivened by people is here his subject, and the busy anecdotal picture conveys that sense of urban excitement of which English literature of the period is so full. 'The happiness of London is not to be conceived but by those who have been in it,' is only one of Johnson's trenchant elogiums, to which Canaletto seems to

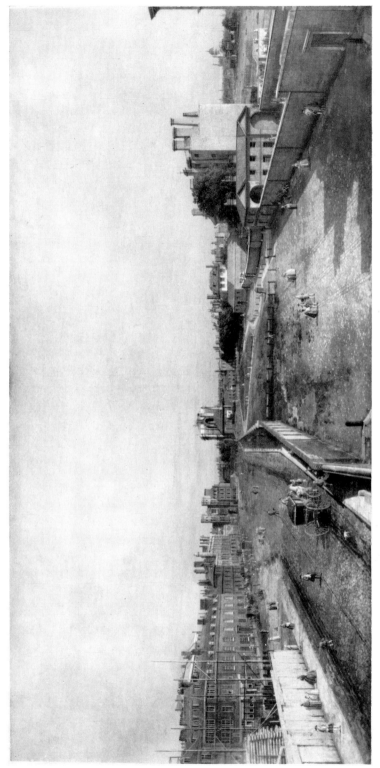

36. ANTONIO CANALETTO: *View of Whitehall*. Duke of Buccleuch collection

subscribe. But his London is not so much Georgian as the more restricted, tighter-ordered London of Queen Anne; his counterpoint of careful light and shade over the bricks of a façade, the cobbles of a street, seems to have all the precision of a couplet by Pope:

> The lights and shades, whose well-accorded strife
> Gives all the strength and colour of our life.

With a Dutch zeal for minutiae Canaletto builds his houses brick by brick, in front a precise line of iron railings, and above, against a dusty lilac sky, a glittering weathercock or the sharp point of a steeple. All this is animated by the bustle of contemporary life: 'Streets, chairs and coxcombs rush upon my sight.' Canaletto is like the diarists of the period, a gossip too in his way, happy in recording day-to-day events, quite unconscious of any larger sphere. His view of nature is always an urban view. Just as Wilde's Gwendolen Fairfax was glad to say she had never seen a spade, so Canaletto would have been glad to say he had never seen a tree; nor, from the sticks of broccoli he puts up as trees, would one suppose he ever had. Once or twice he strays further into nature in the environs of London and paints a cow. There his studies of natural phenomena stop, and it is easy to see why Ruskin got so angry with him. Against Turner Canaletto does seem a mechanical purveyor of mechanically produced views: to the nineteenth century Pope appeared mechanical against Shelley. Yet Turner himself respected Canaletto, and paid him a ludicrously touching homage in that picture *Canaletto painting Venice*, where Canaletto stands in a topographically very inaccurate city working at a gold-framed painting.

Canaletto was about fifty-eight when he finally left London for Venice, after a period of some ten years, on and off, in England. Back home his activity continued ceaselessly. He still was the most celebrated view painter in Italy, still was the 'famous Canaletti' whose pictures visitors bought and brought back. It was not until 1763, however, that prejudice against his type of art softened enough for him to be admitted to the Venetian Academy. And at Rome during the eighteenth century, the Director of the French Academy refused rooms to landscape painters, reserving them for students of that much higher branch of art: history painting.

It was, therefore, tactful of Canaletto, if not obligatory, to present as his *morceau de réception* not a view but an architectural caprice (fig. 37), still in the Accademia at Venice. Here the motifs are not specifically Venetian at all and Canaletto turns back to the theatrical architectural settings of his youth, though sprinkling the scene still with touches of genre—like the woman sitting sewing at the right. There is no obvious effort at fantasy or picturesqueness; the intention is rather to invent an impressive vista in the grand manner, splendidly lit, and based on the dignified principles of perspective. Three of Canaletto's contemporaries practising as view painters followed each other at different periods as official teachers of perspective at the Academy, and this science could be used to elevate the otherwise humble one,

37. ANTONIO CANALETTO: *An Architectural Caprice*. Venice, Accademia

view painting; even at its best that was merely a form of copying and lacked 'invention'. Algarotti had employed Canaletto on those unions of invention and fact which put the Rialto, the Pantheon and some ruins altogether in a caprice setting. Canaletto's *morceau de réception* is something much more ambitious, though not unique in his late work: the creation of a scene which shall appear realistic but which is in fact totally invented. The result, large, elaborate, carefully designed and carefully painted, now seems to us (not surprisingly) academic.

His view pictures did not cease. He continued his *reportage* of Venice, and was

38. ANTONIO CANALETTO: *Piazza S. Marco*. London, National Gallery

occasionally to be found recording the city from life, as it were. While a certain John Crewe and his tutor were staying in Venice in 1760 on the inevitable Grand Tour, they found one morning on the Piazza a little man busily sketching the Campanile; they stopped, and he introduced himself: he was Canaletto. His paintings had become more mannered than ever: tighter in handling, the figures convulsed by a sort of arthritis, with mere blobs for faces. The scale of these late

39. ANTONIO CANALETTO: *The Interior of S. Marco*. Drawing. Hamburg, Kunsthalle

pictures is a good deal smaller than had been usual in pre-London days. In fact, apart from his *morceau de réception*, Canaletto hardly attempted elaborate pictures again, preferring small, often upright canvases, such as the pair in the National Gallery, both views of Piazza San Marco (fig. 38). Whereas X-rays of, for example, the *Stone Mason's Yard* show how he altered the buildings as he painted, an X-ray of one of these two views reveals no alterations or second thoughts at all. From the first everything was painted in as rapidly and neatly and surely as appears on the surface; Canaletto had been so long at the task of view painting that his hand possessed an assuredness which age had not weakened. Certainly he was vain—justifiably—of the ability which time seemed to leave untouched. On a drawing showing the interior of S. Marco (fig. 39) he notes the date 1766, and adds the proud words 'done without spectacles'. The drawing is very careful, almost indeed laboured, full of his late mannerisms but a final testimony to the microscopic accuracy of an artist who had so early been summed up as one whose excellence lay in painting what fell under his eye. Two years later he was dead.

What Carlevaris had adumbrated, Canaletto fully and exhaustively expressed. In the iceblock of his later style, he has marvellously preserved the Venice of his day. His pictures are among the few topographical paintings where accuracy and aesthetic pleasure blend and he created something which even his fellow-artists were forced ultimately to recognize: the view picture as a work of art. An interesting tribute to him is paid by Mrs. Thrale (become Piozzi), who bought seven of his pictures when she went to Venice some years after his death. Discussing Fanny Burney's novel *Cecilia* she speaks of it as a mere picture of topical life, not derived from study. 'Burney's Cecilia is to Richardson's Clarissa,' she goes on 'what a camera obscura in the window of a London parlour—is to a view of Venice by the clear pencil of Canaletti.'

But if only because of his value as a witness, Canaletto was bound to be remembered and to be required. Unlike the history painters in Venice he was at least 'true' and such an exponent of the neo-classic as Angelica Kauffmann owned two 'very fine views' by him. Even in the Romantic period he was not neglected. 'Your own Canalettos' writes Byron's friend Rose to Henry Hallam in 1819, 'will have given you a better idea of the gondola than I could convey. . . .' And in some sense Venice was still his city: 'Avec ses palais, ses gondoles,' Gautier's poem expresses it: 'La ville de Canaletto!'

Although the most famous of the view painters, Canaletto was at no period the sole practitioner in Venice. His own fame attracted others to the subject, and they even imitated his manner as well as his matter. Some of these figures are now hopelessly shadowy; we hear of their names, but can hardly distinguish their works amid the mass of Canalettesque pastiches. A certain Moretti, who was a scene designer, is mentioned and praised by Algarotti for a picture where 'l'auteur a parfaitement imité la manière de Canaletto'—though Algarotti has overpraised his imitative gifts to judge from such Morettis as we know to-day. And there are other more shadowy figures still, while there remains the evidence of activity in those Canalettesque pictures not by Canaletto.

One or two figures, however, are clearly defined personalities who have largely been recovered from oblivion in the last fifty years. Closest to Canaletto is his nephew Bernardo Bellotto (1720–80), who at twenty-seven quitted Venice for Northern Europe never to return: a retreat which is probably a tribute to Canaletto's exclusive grip on the Venetian view painting market. Bellotto began with views of Venice, of Lucca, Padua, even Rome, which counterfeited his uncle's manner as closely as possible—to the annoyance of art historians now working on the problem of which painter painted what. Bellotto's talent was sufficient for a Venetian to note him at twenty-three, with his uncle, both as *rinomatissimi* for view painting. Gradually he drew away from Canaletto's manner, distinguishing his pictures by pinkish sky tones, cold blues and greens of foliage and trees; then he withdrew physically in 1747 to Dresden. His final and most interesting phase was at Warsaw, where during the remaining twelve years of his life he was employed by the unhappy last king of Poland, Stanislas Poniatowski, painting views of the city whose genre qualities seem to prelude Goya and whose strong naturalism is like a breath of the nineteenth century, almost of Courbet (fig. 40). Bellotto no doubt found it convenient to leave Venice but equally he found it convenient to air his association with Canaletto; after his departure he began to sign himself 'Bellotto de Canaletto', and in Poland in fact he was and still is called Canaletto. While his uncle in London was being supposed an impostor, Bellotto was doing his best actually to be an impostor and pass under the more famous name.

Bellotto's retirement from Venice removed one possible rival; another was removed for Canaletto by death. A talented young Venetian, Michiel Marieschi (1710–43), reversed Bellotto's career by returning from Germany to Venice about 1735; previously a scene-designer and painter of harbour scenes and vaguely landscape caprices in Marco Ricci's style, he now turned to view painting. And in 1741 he published a series of twenty-one etched views of Venice.

Marieschi painted few views, though his name is often used to pass off work too indifferent to be by Canaletto and Carlevaris, but the handling of the paint is lively and fresh in a manner of his own. And the people he sets in his views are like those in his earlier work brightly-coloured, vivacious, and with something of Zais's Frenchified elegance. Marieschi's nervous rapid manner is a contrast to Canaletto's at the very moment when that was growing stiff and mechanical. It anticipates Guardi who must have taken some hints from Marieschi, but it is much less calligraphic. His *View of the Rialto* (fig. 41) has a vividness which Canaletto had once possessed, but had lost. Guardi was still working away as history painter. Marieschi's sudden adoption of view painting seems to show that the genre had become popular during his absence in Germany. Perhaps he too would have achieved popularity, if he had not died prematurely. Even as it is, his name occurs frequently in English sale catalogues from about 1760 onwards, and Marshal Schulenburg appears to have been among those at Venice who patronized him.

40. BERNARDO BELLOTTO: *The Church of the Reformed Friars, Warsaw.* Warsaw, National Museum

41. MICHIEL MARIESCHI: *View of the Rialto.* Bristol, City Art Gallery

There were other artists at work, occasionally practising as view painters but more often concerned with perspectives of ruins and architecture: *prospettive* of a type that really go back to the Renaissance and to the ideal cities painted and planned by Piero della Francesca. In these pictures the figures were occasionally by another hand—even Tiepolo, at Algarotti's request, painted small figures into some ruin-pieces. Among the minor men at work, Gian Francesco Costa alone actually created a new subject matter by depicting—in a series of etchings—scenes outside Venice: the villas of Venetian nobles along the Brenta canal. In one or two etchings Canaletto had strayed outside a city (usually Padua), but Costa's *Delizie del fiume Brenta* were really an extension of the topographical etchings of Carlevaris, and a glorification of Venetian aristocracy. The sumptuous villas had impressed an early English traveller, Bishop Burnet; they are palaces rather than villas and, as he says, 'built with so great a variety of architecture that there is not one of them like another.' No doubt Ruskin never heard of Costa but he knew the villas well enough, passing them as so many travellers still do on the road between Padua and Venice, and they too earned a sneer: 'This is the architecture to which her studies of the Renaissance have conducted modern Italy.' Once again, in such remarks, the nineteenth century sets out to demolish its prosaic wicked old father: the eighteenth century.

The humblest rivals of Canaletto, or perhaps rather his copyists, decorated such eternally Venetian souvenirs as fans with festival scenes, usually the Ascension Day ceremony. Cheaper and more portable than a picture, these tourist products probably followed the vogue that Canaletto had virtually created; and in a way the idea behind the picture and the fan is the same. Only a few views are to be found on porcelain of the period, perhaps in part because there was little export of it. Some *capricci* do occur, but these are anyway more usually based on standard Delft designs than on anything specifically Venetian.

Canaletto's great successor was to come to view painting comparatively late. Francesco Guardi certainly inherited the tradition of Canaletto and patronage by the English, but achieved something quite different. The informative Strange, patron himself of Guardi, supplies a fragment of explanation in his catalogue: 'Guardi is a painter still living at Venice; and who, though he has taken Canaletto's department, has still followed a particular manner; which is spirited and quite his own.' The truth is that Guardi lacked the technical mastery to imitate Canaletto very closely, even if he wished to. Although he began by imitation of it, he was actually a rebel against the Canalettesque set-piece of hard light and shade, complicated composition and elaborate theatrical perspective.

His creation was more personal and more truly capricious. Canaletto's static scene was replaced by an evocation more of fantasy than fact, in which nothing is ever quite still. Strong contrasts of light and shade are softened to a suffused pale glow which bathes the whole picture; the composition itself is often stripped of

42. ANTONIO CANALETTO: *View towards Murano.* Windsor Castle.
Reproduced by gracious permission of H.M. The Queen

people and buildings until there is no more to it but a stretch of water and a single gondola under the empty atmospheric sky. The bold copperplate of Canaletto's calligraphy is dismissed in favour of an erratic and flickering scrawl. A bomb has exploded softly in the middle of Canaletto's careful constructions; they are broken up, just as the compositions of Titian had been broken up by Tintoretto. And in the touches of splintered light with which Tintoretto heightened his figures and scenes we see a source for Guardi's figure painting—and his view painting.

Guardi's career as a figure painter had been shared with his brother Gian Antonio, and has already been discussed. In 1760 Gian Antonio died, and very probably about that date Guardi began his view painting. Then in 1764 the diarist Gradenigo noted that he had exhibited in Piazza San Marco two views commissioned by an Englishman; it is Gradenigo who glosses the name Guardi with the phrase 'good pupil of the famous Canaletto'. Since Guardi was very rarely referred to by his contemporaries during some thirty years of view painting, the reference is the more valuable. Whether it should be taken literally to mean that Guardi had really been a pupil of Canaletto is a vexed point; Guardi did many times copy Canaletto designs—just as Canaletto had copied those of Carlevaris—and his earliest views are certainly the closest echo of Canaletto's handling which he can manage. These pictures are straggly attempts at architecture, with a few scratchy figures littering the untidy scene. But already there are signs of Guardi's later development in the vivacity of these figures; they prophesy freedom, even as do the wavering black outlines of the buildings, from the straitjacket of Canaletto's style.

Soon Guardi replaced his own flat and dull blue skies by an awareness of light and shade which seemed a return to Canaletto's early manner: thundery effects which had long ceased to appear in view pictures. Just how near the two artists could come is illustrated by a *View of Murano* (fig. 42) now in the Royal Collection at Windsor. This has usually been attributed to Canaletto, and if so, must be a very early work in his most free manner; more than once, however, the hypothesis has been put forward that the picture is in fact by Guardi—an idea actually more tempting than likely. Admittedly, this is a unique example of such confusion, for Guardi's weaknesses usually betray themselves most when he imitates Canaletto, one reason for refusing to accept this fine painting as his.

What Guardi's comparatively early views were like is conveyed on an unusually grand scale by the *Basin of St. Mark's* (fig. 43) where the Canalettesque idiom is apparent but has now been partly absorbed by Guardi's greater vivacity. The untidy effect is the untidiness of Venice, of boats and rigging and seamen. Already his sensitive awareness of atmosphere can be appreciated and his frank delight in the marine world of his adopted city. His later pictures simplify subject-matter in contrast to the busy scene here, but sky and water remain his real subject; Venice raises its façades and towers almost tentatively into this stormy atmospheric world where the elements buffet what man has built.

It was in the caprice view where Canaletto had so often failed that Guardi so splendidly succeeded. But with Guardi the caprice became much less obviously— and clumsily—a juxtaposition of various monuments. Inspired by the ruins on islands in the Venetian Lagoon (often the old fortifications of the city now fallen into decay), he painted ruin-pieces half real and half imaginary, in which it is difficult to say quite what is invented. These ruin-pieces are barely melancholy; rather are they enchanted archways and weed-overgrown pillars poised against a pale sky and about to lapse into the pale water. The century loved such effects; its taste for ruins had been decorative and partly architectural (resulting in the capricious ruin-pieces assembled by Marco Ricci) and finally became sentimental. What

43. FRANCESCO GUARDI: *The Basin of S. Marco.* Waddesdon Manor, Aylesbury, National Trust (Rothschild Bequest)

44. FRANCESCO GUARDI: *A Caprice Landscape.*
Almelo, H. E. ten Cate collection

was, for instance, evoked in Diderot by ruin-pieces was almost a nostalgia: 'Tout s'anéantit, tout périt, tout passe.'

Guardi's pictures seem a part of that taste; but they are also seascapes as well as evocative *capricci*, and he was the first painter to look outside the city of Venice and to paint the water that lay around it. He seems to have had an instinctive gift for transposing literal topography into scenes which have a poetic reality even while clearly in part fantasies. A view like fig. 44 at first sight looks like a scene on an island in the lagoon, but is full of romantic half-invented elements such as the arch at the left and the Palladian building behind. In no pejorative sense, this blended truth and fiction is 'picturesque': the house in the centre, itself so ravishingly painted, becomes an object of romance, and the washing hung out from it to dry is like some mysterious signal in a fairy-tale. Even the activity of the tiny figures remains mysterious, as they rush about ant-like, enlivening the scene. From the first Guardi perhaps intended to *interpret* Venice rather than *reproduce* it, and his best views of it capture a sparkle of light and a sense of eternal movement which Canaletto never caught, and which is certainly part of the city. The ubiquitous water of Venice, mirroring palaces and bridges, receiving the slowly subsiding foundations of stone and rotting wood, is evoked in its flash and ripples and ready movement.

Canaletto had devoted himself to painting each ripple as if it were a brick on a façade. But Canaletto was the product of an earlier period and kept always something of Flemish prosaicism before the extravagant spectacle of Venice. As the century advanced, the tendency was towards lightness and grace: asymmetry replaced symmetry, not only in furniture and books but even in the detail of the decoration of Venetian visiting cards (on which *capricci* often appear). Whether or not we care to call it rococo, this new grace and airiness was at work expanding the bubble of late eighteenth-century Venice before it finally burst. Guardi had an example personally close at hand in his brother-in-law, Tiepolo, whose own style shows the same progression from darkness into light and whose silvery landscape backgrounds have affinities with Guardi.

This mood perhaps suited visitors to Venice during the last two decades before the fall of the Republic: in those years when Venice could no longer conceal from itself its degradation and decay. This was the time when the Doge could refer in a speech to the Senate to the many difficulties of the day, the contemporary inertia, the languor, the mental and physical sluggishness of the nation; and that speech was meant as a defence of Venetian policy. There were many sympathizers with French thought, the more prominent of whom were in these years arrested and imprisoned. Such priests who attempted to take the part of the people against the nobles found themselves equally accused; there were, however, few of them. While Guardi evoked more and more airy caprices where the ruins have hardly more solidity than clouds and the clouds themselves are pale breaths on the horizon, Venetians began gradually to replace religion by rationalism. Cases arose of workers who were reported as believing only what they saw; at Murano the State Inquisitors in 1779 reported, for example, a glass worker who thought the soul merely air which was exhaled at death. And two years before, a liberal Venetian had presented Voltaire with a medal showing Philosophy overthrowing Superstition.

At Venice the Carnival continued but the gambling place, the Ridotto, had closed. Visitors came as frequently and as numerously as ever to the city; its attractions did not pall, the automatic cycle of its annual feasts went its course—though religious feasts were diminished in number in 1787—and Guardi painted. Canaletto's late paintings had been on an unusually small scale—for him—and now Guardi specialized in small pictures, flickering enchantments of ruins along islands in the Venetian Lagoon or a roofless hall set against a breezy sky of blue and white, sometimes painted on wood hardly larger than a matchbox: pictures which when framed in the delicate gilded frames of the period must have seemed more trinkets than proper paintings (fig. 45).

With time his style increased in allusiveness. The people who had played such a

45. FRANCESCO GUARDI: *Caprices with Ruins*. London, National Gallery

part in Canaletto's pictures, even when given only the mechanical vivacity of puppets, dwindled in Guardi's work until they were mere specks of colour, a running squiggle of white paint, a black dot, short-hand to express the population of the most moribund of European states. Canaletto had always liked to introduce some touch of genre—a man with his steaming coffee cup as in that view of the Piazza (fig. 38), or the woman sewing in his *morceau de réception* (fig. 37), but on the tiny scale of Guardi's late pictures there is no room for such personalities. Animation is general, and the effect is rather like that which Dufy gave to his paintings of events. Like Dufy, Guardi often achieves a sort of spontaneous wit. Where Canaletto had been particular and specific, Guardi was content with a hieroglyphic symbol. In Canaletto there are nearly always small passages of delicate but solid painting enlivening vast areas of mechanical topography: the stretched yellow silk of a sunshade or the white icing-hard silhouette of a statue against blue sky.

Such detail has no place in Guardi's paintings, where the oil paint is in fact often diluted to almost water-colour thinness; the view is glimpsed in a single *coup d'œil*, becoming almost an impression. This 'impressionism' has sometimes led to the idea that Guardi anticipated the French Impressionists (whose views of Venice are mostly so bad) and Turner. But Guardi's handling is really an inspired accident rather than a scientific method of vision, and his attitude to Venice is neither romantic nor sentimental. He never heightens the shimmering nobility of Venice to make it the dream city of Turner's pictures; his Venice is slightly raffish, lop-sided, now noble, now squalid. It is true that he seems to express a fresh awareness of atmospheric effects and already to agree with Constable's remark that the best lesson he ever had was 'Remember light and shade never stand still'. But Guardi's love of movement, of pale tones and luminous skies, is based less on naturalism than on the heightened rococo of his century: its love of lightness, elegance, and grace.

To his period he was an unimportant view painter and no doubt it would be amazed at his fame to-day. Such patronage as he received cannot have made him very rich. Little is recorded about who patronized him and an example of employing him on the sort of thing which really suited his talent least seems to have been Thomas Moore Slade's commission given about 1775. Of this we hear that the result was a 'Bird's eye View of all Venice. Composed and painted for Mr. Slade'. Whereas Canaletto could charge a hundred sequins or more for a picture, Guardi (it is said) charged one. There was probably no Guardi studio in which assistants could prepare pictures which the master finished—only Guardi's incompetent son Giacomo (1764–1835), who later specialized in gouache views of Venice often derived from his father, but without any of Francesco's sparkle. To-day even Giacomo's gouaches have come into favour and we have eclipsed even the eighteenth and early nineteenth centuries in our passion for Venice and Venetian pictures. A good number of his father's pictures seem to have been left on Giacomo's hands, and he probably made a little money by trading these; one or two of them were bought from him by a priest at Ancona from whom they were later acquired for an English collector and so arrived in this country.

It is a picture such as the *Tower of Malghera* (fig. 46) which shows us Guardi at his most personal in a straight-forward view. The tower itself, which was destroyed in the nineteenth century, was a relic of the ancient Venetian fortifications on an island in the Lagoon; Canaletto had used it as motif in one of his etchings, but Guardi does not depend upon that. He clears his composition of all that Canaletto would have filled it with, and achieves a Corot-esque simplicity. The painting is all sky and water, and the thin crisp shell of the foreground boat with its graceful arc of mast emphasizes the space of the picture. It is a grey-blue atmosphere, a tone painting in which drawing is kept to a minimum—at the right a few hasty scratches with the brush's point serve to evoke a bit of land and hint at another boat.

In such pictures Guardi seems to dismiss all the eighteenth century's interest in mankind and attempt a purer type of landscape for its own sake than had been attempted before. Certainly such a change was realized at the time; whether it was appreciated is a different matter. When Strange writes of Guardi from England to

I

46. FRANCESCO GUARDI: *The Tower of Malghera*. London, National Gallery

his Venetian agent Sasso it is to warn him that Guardi needs watching: the painter must not be allowed to follow his fancy but must stick to the truth. Strange is going to order from Guardi two more views which must be clear, well-executed, and a pair, but also coloured *exactly*—Strange's italics. That is the voice of the eighteenth-century English patron.

In the last years of his long life—*vedute* painters seem to have enjoyed longevity—Guardi, almost like Gainsborough, escaped from reproductions of reality into fancy pictures where he could be his own master, and into little rapid luminous sketches in oil paint which hit off Venice without attempting to be 'well-executed' as Strange used the words. He really could not help his lyrical gift for transcribing reality in his own highly personal terms, and his many drawings show this spontaneous freedom almost better than his pictures. In his drawings he need please only himself. Spontaneity, sketch-like character, evocation rather than steady realism, these are the virtues which the eighteenth century did not easily pardon in Gainsborough, nor the nineteenth century in Constable. Both painters were too free; Gainsborough refused to conform and Constable conformed only in his big public pictures which our taste now finds so dull and lifeless. Guardi does not seem to have been deterred too much—and we are the gainers. With the coming of the nineteenth century he became more popular; it was only unfortunate that he was already dead. Then his name fell into oblivion, and was hardly revived again seriously until George Simonson wrote a pioneer monograph, still the standard work, in 1904.

Guardi nearly, but not quite, lived to see the fall of the Republic. He died in 1793. The duration of Venice's enchanted life was speedily coming to an end: the burning of the *bucintoro*, the theft of the Horses of S. Marco. But his views kept until the finish a gaiety and a busy vivacity which are now almost ironic. Four years later the Senate resolved to accept the provisional government of Napoleon; the Doge abdicated and shortly after died.

Venice survived as a city, however, and view painting too did not quite cease. It staggered on inevitably, as the demand did not slacken. Canaletto's and Guardi's changed hands, and when there were no originals available imitations of both painters answered the demand. One of the most successful combiners of the two styles, a postscript himself to that century, was Giovanni Migliara (1785–1837), whose work is interesting for the divided homage he paid to the twin poles of Venetian view painting.

It was science not politics which destroyed the view painter's livelihood and made his art redundant. The camera was invented.

IV

GENRE

PIETRO Longhi (1702–85) virtually *is* genre painting in Venice for the major portion of the century. Although by no means a great or good painter, he did manage to invent a sub-division of the genre picture which had not previously existed there and which died with him. Painters, like other people, must have their antecedents; Longhi of course had his, but less than with most painters do they satisfactorily explain what he invented and what he achieved. He might almost be said to be, despite his deficiencies, the Jane Austen of Venetian eighteenth-century art, content with a few inches of canvas and managing to convey within that deliberately limited area a vivid, unique aspect of his city and his age.

He did not, however, begin as a genre painter. Trained under Balestra, he began first with figure painting for which he was to remain unsuited. At intervals throughout his career he continued to practise as figure painter: frescoing a ceiling in Palazzo Sagredo and some religious scenes in S. Pantaleon, and executing occasional poor oil paintings of historical or religious subjects. Balestra seems to have recognized Longhi's unsuitability for any of that type of work and he sent him off instead to Giuseppe Maria Crespi (1665–1747) at Bologna. While Longhi was to remain very much a private and unpublicized phenomenon of Venice, Crespi was a painter patronized by Popes, foreign princes and Italian princes beyond Bologna. As well as portraits and subject-pieces, he did practise a sort of genre painting; and his *Family Group* (fig. 47), which is of himself and his family, is a good example of the confused but intimate manner of his genre work which must have provided Longhi with at least some useful hints. This picture itself was not available for Longhi to see, as it had been given by the painter to Grand Prince Ferdinand de' Medici at Florence in 1708. In point of fact it was a good deal more vivid and intimate than Longhi ever cared to be, and it is an impression of domestic reality that remained altogether unusual in Italy.

Outside Venice but throughout Northern Italy there had for long existed a tradition of genre which took its subjects deliberately from low life. The origins of this type of painting are obscure, but its products are many; it certainly played its part in Crespi's development and through Crespi it influenced at Venice Piazzetta as well as Longhi. Not content with low life subjects, it chose to emphasize the disgusting, sordid and sickly side of them whenever it could. There can be little doubt that the great attraction of such pictures, and the pleasure they gave, was—and is—sexual. That taste for dirty washing which impels Zola to such elaborate physical

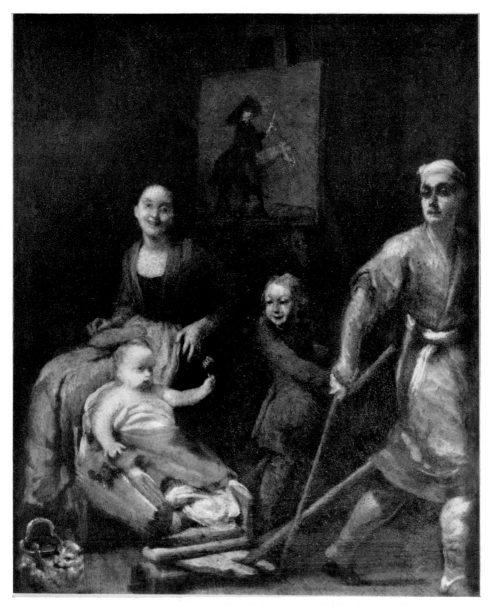

47. GIUSEPPE MARIA CRESPI: *The Painter and his Family*. Florence, Uffizi

descriptions of soiled laundry in *L'Assommoir*, in Italy found its pleasure in flea-ridden peasant girls and seductively ragged urchins whose clothes and persons promised a good dose of *nostalgie de boue*. Such a painter as Giacomo Ceruti, wandering about Northern Italy in the first half of the eighteenth century, added his own twist to such subjects by choosing often to make his peasants and scavengers diseased, while proclaiming his own unpleasant pre-occupations by the browns and

48. GIACOMO CERUTI: *Two Poor Men*. Brescia, Pinacoteca Tosio Martinengo

yellows in which he painted. All grotesques are obscene fundamentally, as is the taste which finds them either funny or appealing: the stunted and afflicted people of Ceruti, as we see them in his *Two Poor Men* (fig. 48), are a sharp reminder of how uncivilized the supposedly civilized Italian eighteenth century could be. They are people painted without sympathy, without even the romanticism of Murillo or the prosaic humanity of the Dutch seventeenth-century artists.

Longhi did not remain quite indifferent to this sort of art, as it reached him through Crespi. Crespi had occasionally taken a single peasant figure, perhaps a girl searching herself for fleas, and placed it in a plain shadowy setting, very much as Longhi did in some of his early pictures, like the *Peasant Girl* (fig. 49), which is close in style to the pictures produced by Piazzetta after his apprenticeship to Crespi. Longhi's girl is not at all disgusting; she is, rather, healthy and alluring—at least by intention—and is painted in soft, vague brush strokes that show a good deal of affinity with Crespi's work.

This picture is a timid exercise in genre of a kind not really sympathetic to Longhi. He is here following a vogue which he does not properly understand; it was

49. PIETRO LONGHI: *A Peasant Girl*. Bassano, Museo Civico

to be left to Piazzetta to take up Crespi's people and make of them something quite novel. Longhi, untrained by his training under Balestra and not properly orientated by working with Crespi, arrived back in Venice in the autumn of 1732 (if not before) and soon after began the long series of domestic and public Venetian scenes by which we know him best.

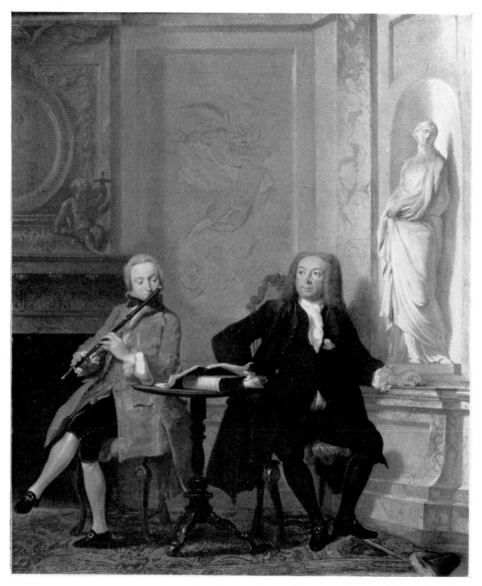

50. CORNELIS TROOST: *Two Dilettanti*. Dublin, National Gallery of Ireland

Although the invention of such work at Venice seems to be Longhi's own, the taste of other cities and countries was also independently turning towards private life interiors often similar to Longhi's, though technically much better. In Holland the painter Cornelis Troost had already embarked on his career, and a picture like his *Dilettanti* (fig. 50), painted in 1736, is already a vivid combination of personalities and surroundings: a tribute, even if a mildly satiric one, to new conceptions of civilized ease. It is at once dignified, cultured and informal; the setting is min-

51. PIETRO LONGHI: *A Concert*. Venice, Accademia

utely particularized, as are the costumes, and we are shown a private moment of music-making—in its way as personal as somebody singing in his bath. Troost of course had a long and distinguished ancestry in painters of interiors like Vermeer and de Hoogh, and he also is respectful to the actual medium of paint which he handles until it resembles enamel. The picture is finished and neat, and charming partly because of its intense clarity.

Longhi's *Concert* (fig. 51), painted five years later and the first dated domestic scene by him that we know of, is vivid enough but depressingly clumsy; even his musicians seem to lack the quick-fingered deftness of Troost's amateur flautist. The paint surface is messy, as so often in Longhi; time and practice never taught him how to apply paint. But despite the clumsy drawing and the totally unorganized composition, there is a perhaps greater talent for lively observation than Troost was ever capable of and a greater vivacity through the very spontaneous slap-dash paint. And while Troost was drawn away into painting scenes from harlequinades and plays, Longhi was to devote virtually his whole production to scenes of contemporary life like this one. There is a sort of candour in the slightly ridiculous trio of musical amateurs and a sort of pungency in the pair of clerical card-players, one thin and eager, the other fat and porcinely benevolent.

The suggestions of unorganization in the scene, both as a composition and as a subject, are typical of Longhi and raise the question of whether he was naïve or just falsely naïve. He is a painter whose current fate is to receive the most extravagant and obtuse praise which can be given, even by Italian critics, to an artist. Where every clumsiness is supposed a touch of genius, and where Longhi is coupled with Watteau (to be fair, this dreadful analogy was started by Mariette) and paragoned with Renoir or Manet, it is not likely that he will be appreciated justly or reasonably. Because he is unique it has been presumed that he is invaluable. But it seems as if his clumsy handling of paint, his inability ever to establish the planes of a picture, and his incapacity to draw properly, were honest defects that he could not overcome even after many years of practice.

His pictures are therefore, with all their undoubted charm, lazy little pictures: just as the society he pictures is lazy. The world he sees is in general the enclosed one of affluent people trying to pass the time. The rooms they inhabit are enclosed too, and always windowless; they themselves are barely in contact with each other but are placed, like dolls, in a proximity physical rather than emotional. *The Visit* (fig. 52), of only a few years after the *Concert*, is like an illustration of the theme of vapidity; one feels the man at the left bends down to welcome with relief the lively frisking dog—the sole lively creature in the room. But this is already reading too much significance into Longhi. Although his aristocrats seem to linger aimlessly over their toilet or sip their coffee wearily, they are not observed with any of the biting irony that Parini was to use in indicting high society in his set of poems *Il Giorno*. Outside Venice social conditions occupied the thoughts of Italians and other Europeans. Before Parini, Pietro Verri at Milan had satirized various aspects of contemporary life: from absurd social prejudices to the sort of education girls were given in finishing schools. At Milan a whole enlightened group of people existed, publishing a journal *Il Caffè* (modelled on the *Spectator*) and in it vigorously denouncing the idleness of the nobility and the state of the country. From out of the ideas of that group came Beccaria's famous proposals for the abolition of

52. PIETRO LONGHI: *The Visit*. New York, Metropolitan Museum

capital punishment—a treatise which the Venetian State hastened to have refuted by a tame priestly pamphleteer.

Longhi does not run counter to the Venetian climate of the period; nothing accuses or upsets the placidity of his people, so conscious of their elegance and so assured of their charm. It is not surprising that he was a painter much patronized by the Venetian aristocracy. By 1748 he is found writing that it is difficult to borrow his own pictures (required for a project of engraving some) as they are chiefly in noble households; and he is recorded as working for families like the Grimani, the Pisani and the Sagredo (for whom he also acted once as picture valuer). It is through engravings that he is mentioned in England—for the first time (?)—in 1750: by Vertue who calls him 'Petri Lungi'. By 1753 we hear from an Italian source that his pictures fetch *grossi prezzi*.

As well as pictures of his betters, he painted in the same intimate calm manner scenes of Venetian low life, low without being vulgar. These are often street scenes, airless as had been his interiors, set against a plain wall or under the arcades of the Ducal Palace, and emphasizing some picturesque aspect of Venetian life. He records thus the various animals brought to Venice at carnival times, perhaps the most exciting of which was the rhinoceros which arrived for the carnival of 1751. It was centuries since a rhinoceros had been seen in Europe; Dürer had recorded the last specimen and now the arrival of a new one created a sensation so great that one of the distinguished scholars of the day, Scipione Maffei, solemnly set down his thoughts on the subject in a pamphlet. Other animals might be popular, but this was the most popular of all; Longhi painted the subject at least twice, and pupils or imitators painted it more often. And Alessandro Longhi, Pietro's son, engraved yet another composition of it. Then it went off to Verona, where once again it was sketched.

After this hubbub the poor creature seems tame enough, as it placidly stands with a wisp of straw in its mouth (fig. 53). Its journey from Africa via Nuremburg to Venice is perhaps a symbol: something primitive and grotesque coming from that continent so long thought of as productive of novelties, and being welcomed as 'a change'. There is an element of sadness and futility in the onlookers; the rhinoceros once seen, there remains no more entertainment to be extracted from it, and despite the gesticulating showman his crowd seem already to have exhausted their emotions of wonder and surprise.

Hogarth (Longhi has been compared to Hogarth) would have wrung something savagely satiric out of such a scene, sympathizing with the beast or with the on-lookers. There would have been, in brief, a point to the picture above the mere record-making task of painting what the rhinoceros looked like. Goya (Longhi has been compared to Goya) would have seized like a bird of prey upon the very vacuity of the people he had to depict, enjoying their emptiness as a child enjoys the emptiness of a balloon: he could have blown it out to monstrous swollen pro-portions. Longhi no doubt had to tread more carefully at Venice, while at the same time his mind had shown neither desire nor ability to express anything other than what it registered as *seen*.

What there was for him to see often, fortunately, possessed charm and attractive-ness and even a simple harmless humour. So he managed to invest his pictures with

53. PIETRO LONGHI: *The Rhinoceros*. Venice, Ca' Rezzonico

those qualities *trouvés*. He was popular with his contemporaries because of the mirror he held up to the nature all around them. Gradenigo records that he is the painter *per attitudini naturali* and for *parlanti caricature*. Gasparo Gozzi thought that Longhi could usefully and suitably be compared with Giambattista Tiepolo; for him Longhi was a painter who had evolved from scenes of figures dressed up in historical costume and who, instead of imagining how people looked, painted what he saw 'with his own eyes'. That was Gozzi's own talent too—not for nothing was he a journalist and a witty critic of contemporary manners; his 'own eyes' noted the behaviour of crowds on the Piazza S. Marco, or followed, with the rest of Gozzi, a pair of modern lovers whose antics struck him as diverting. And Gozzi went out of his way to say that Longhi's kind of art was no whit inferior to Tiepolo's.

Gozzi's attitude is a sign of the times: that people were beginning more and more to tire of imaginative painting and its themes of gods and goddesses and heroes and hero-worship. What concerned the age more intimately was itself. At one level records of its daily existence were prized in themselves: memoirs and journals and diaries, engravings of state occasions and of street cries too, plays of contemporary life with characters often recognizably derived from well-known living people. In place of *opera seria*, the 'Beggar's Opera' was preferred. Grimm, for instance, who certainly preferred the latter, pointedly remarked of those deities from machines who had made such frequent appearances in opera, 'Un dieu peut étonner, mais peut-il intéresser?' A new tendency is crisply expressed there.

Eighteenth-century Venice proliferated with forms of self-presentation, wrapped in a fantasy existence in which it was still a proud and powerful republic. The amount of detail crammed into their pictures by the view painters is almost neurotic, but the Venice they delineated was a public city. Longhi's care is to take us behind the crumbling palace façades, into rooms where the sun never strikes; everything he sees there is minutely and carefully observed, and his drawings (fig. 54) show what meticulous attention he paid to details of furniture and ornaments. His drawings show him also a rather more capable artist. In cases where a drawing can be checked against the final painting, there is nearly always a loss of inspiration in the latter, a fumbling from which the drawing was free.

Outside Venice the eighteenth century was profoundly occupied by morality, and it was increasingly on a moral level that the century interpreted works of art which were records of itself. For painters like Hogarth and Goya, their art is a trenchant comment on their age; not content with seeing with their own eyes, they also utilize their brains. Longhi never risked any comment on his age, if we except one mildly satiric picture of the clergy, and it is significant that Gradenigo should speak of his *parlanti caricature* when he probably means no more than topical allusiveness and vivid depiction of fashions and manners. Satiric pictures were certainly not very well received and an unfortunate Veronese artist (himself a Franciscan) who had the lively idea of painting the four classes of his Order as the four seasons found himself banished to an obscure monastery, after complaints had been made at Venice.

In a very much quoted sonnet Goldoni hailed Longhi as his counterpart in painting, and in a slightly less quoted passage he praised Longhi for having found a

54. PIETRO LONGHI: *Furniture and Figures*. Drawing. Venice, Museo Correr

new way of expressing in pictures 'the character and passions of men'. Goldoni's praise is more interesting as revealing, once more, Longhi's fortunate position at the period than for any inherent truth. Literary men often seize on non-existent parallels in painting, as Diderot stooped to praise Greuze. No doubt Goldoni was pleased by the aptness of Longhi's pictures which do indeed seem to offer the play-wright a widely representative group of *dramatis personæ*—but no plot. Even the innocuous quality of Longhi's scenes would not disturb Goldoni, whose own nature was of the least progressive or revolutionary. Like a good citizen he saw that the Republic should be careful not to offend, for example, its source of revenue—tourists—and he wrote a pamphlet of protest against the satire of Chiari's play *School for Widows* which was full of wounding references to Protestants and to the English. Had Longhi ever permitted himself comment of that nature his fate would perhaps have been similar to Chiari's (and Goldoni's, too): from 1749 onwards all comedies had to be submitted to the Venetian equivalent of the Lord Chamberlain before they might be performed, and doubtless a form of censorship could have been invented for paintings.

Longhi never incurred that risk. He remained content to the last with his own way of recording life about him; his style of painting did not change either, and there is no trace of evolution in his work. Engravings after his pictures executed at the time are one testimony to his popularity, and the number of Longhi-pastiches from the same period are another. In his limited field he remained the master. His official career was considerably more distinguished than, for instance, that of any view painter; he was a founder member of the Venetian Academy, and also an instructor there, as well as being head of the academy of art founded by the Pisani family. He lived long enough to attend the session of the Venetian Academy which elected the young Canova, and long enough to see the major part of his son Alessandro's successful career as portrait painter.

While Pietro Longhi represents genre painting as it appealed to aristocratic Venetian taste, there also existed one or two other much humbler essays in genre. Hardly to be ranked as pictures at all are the series of semi-votive panels which showed the various trades and professions at Venice and which were set up in the offices controlling trading in the city, those of the *Giustizia Vecchia*. The building was placed, suitably enough, near to the centre for the humbler trades' activity, the Rialto. The *Giustizia* was concerned with barbers, tailors and so on; each of these guilds had long before the eighteenth century deposited a panel showing their own trade at work, often with some saintly protector beaming down approvingly from the clouds above. During the eighteenth century the earlier panels were not replaced but were repainted, as inscriptions on them record. One such, *ristaurato* in 1750, shows a rosary shop (fig. 55) and has been converted into pure eighteenth-century genre with its periwigged customer being shown a handful of ornamental rosaries. The picture has been rightly connected with the two Guardi brothers, who either together or individually painted one or two other genre pieces, sometimes taking— in their magpie way—the design from Pietro Longhi, as for other pictures they took from Tiepolo and a whole range of history painters.

The *Rosary Shop* associates the trade, as usual in these panels, with Venice, and the picture is rather like an offering made at a shrine, a sort of token in the hope of continued patronage. At the same time it is part of the extensive representation of everyday life in eighteenth-century Venice, and for this reason the earlier scene was 'restored' and brought up to date in 1750. A further development of this aspect of genre was the collection of drawings by Gaetano Zompini (1700–78), an otherwise quite uninteresting provincial artist, of the various traders and hawkers who went their rounds in Venice. Zompini was living poor and obscure at Venice, and it was apparently at the suggestion of Zanetti that he made these drawings, which were later engraved and published in a book, *Le Arti che vanno per via nella Città di Venezia* (1753). Some rather equivalent 'Street Cries' had been drawn by Amigoni when in England (and engraved by his pupil Wagner). He painted one or two genre pictures, too, including an 'English sweep chimney boy' which does not appear to have been seen by anyone since Dr. Burney saw it in Farinelli's villa outside Bologna.

K

55. GIAN ANTONIO GUARDI(?): *A Rosary Shop*. Venice, Ca' Rezzonico

A ingrassar orti, e vigne schena, e brazzi
Me sporco, e stracco; e porto via scoazze:
E sta nette per mi case, e palazzi.

4

56. GAETANO ZOMPINI: *A Manure Collector*. Engraving

Zompini seems to have felt considerable sympathy, and affinity perhaps, with the rather sad people he drew: lugging their baskets of coal or poultry, selling clothes or telling fortunes. One or two scenes show masked carnival figures, but the theme of the book is an everyday, indeed workaday, Venice, seen at every season of the year in the lives of those perambulating tradespeople whom Zompini drew so badly and yet with a clumsy, forceful actuality (fig. 56). Their lives were not picturesque, nor does Zompini try to pretend they were. In December, 1779, Carlo Contarini spoke publicly in the Great Council on the state of Venice and the plight of the ordinary people. He was angry and rhetorical, but his speech evokes Zompini's world—or rather, a stratum of society below that. Those gay masked figures so dear to the tourist and to Italian historians, passed by night other figures sleeping on the stones of the bridges: figures, Contarini declared, of whom it was not possible to be sure if they were citizens of the Venetian Republic or stray animals. To understand how dangerous comment of this nature was, it is enough to note that Contarini was later arrested and the Inquisitors instrumental in his arrest were declared to have deserved well of the Republic. So the failure of eighteenth-century Venice to produce any open painted comment upon the state of the city and society was not quite an accident; the artists, unconsciously perhaps, conspired with the government to agree to ignore certain things and to emphasize others. In a metaphor, the band played louder to drown the pistol shots.

Isolated from the topicality of Longhi and Longhi's imitators, Piazzetta pursued a very different idea of genre which probably found more patrons among foreigners than Venetians. In the years when Longhi was just starting his proper career, Piazzetta was withdrawing further into his private world with its melancholia and its long delays. His training under Crespi—a much younger Crespi than the rather imperious old figure known to Longhi—had probably only accentuated his feeling for a special kind of realism. And, as he was a Venetian, his 'realism' was tinged with a certain fantasy that gives his best genre pieces an extraordinary poetry. Just as Tiepolo is always the conforming genius of the period, so Piazzetta is the non-conformist; Tiepolo was brilliantly speedy in work, Piazzetta neurotically slow; Tiepolo was in the light and of the light, Piazzetta amid the gloom and obviously hugging the gloom.

The same patrons who commissioned from him altarpieces for churches would retain his genre pictures for their private collections. Thus the Elector of Cologne, Clemens August, through whom Piazzetta's altarpieces reached Germany, had some ten genre pieces, chiefly heads, acquired for himself. For such heads, either painted or drawn, Piazzetta seems to have fused fact and imagination; his boys in exotic fur caps and his sulky peasant girls are recognizably of a type that is Piazzettesque rather than, in any way, *real*. They seem to have only the faintest connection with either Venice or the eighteenth century. They belong really in a timeless world even while they are genre, and in his large pictures in this vein Piazzetta went further to emphasize their bizarreness and their lack of 'reality'.

For another foreign patron, Marshal Schulenburg, Piazzetta painted about 1740 a pair of large genre subjects unique at the period and, perhaps by accident, a last thunderous blow against the increasing light and grace of young painters. The so-called *Idyll* (fig. 57) which is taking place, or is supposed to be taking place, on the seashore, has no subject which can be defined and yet is clearly not a piece of 'real life'. The picture's mystery is increased by its being slightly worn and also possibly unfinished. Where is the seashore and what are these people clad in anachronistic costume doing? The cow's head at the right is also in need of being explained.

Such a picture is really a fantasy, a *capriccio*, on a genre theme. The actual 'subject' of the picture is for us to supply, rather as in certain paintings by Picasso like the *Saltimbanques*, where a group of travelling players stand in a deserted land-scape. That picture made a powerful and haunting impression on Rilke who based a poem upon it. Like Picasso's picture, Piazzetta's seems to raise the urgent question of identity: of the people we look at, and then of ourselves. Again, like the *Saltim-banques*, the *Idyll* seems to preserve a single moment of time while the boy gestic-ulates to attract our attention, and it too has an element of wistfulness and evane-scence. These are people 'a little more fleeting than we ourselves'. In Piazzetta's painting, with its sombre reddish tones that make the figures seem as if lit by firelight, we are free to imagine any combination of circumstances which has tem-porarily brought together these four people and the cow. For the painter it is enough to emphasize the charm and the incongruity of the group, and there is a touch of mysterious poetry in the figure of the girl with the parasol who turns her back and gazes into the turquoise patch of sky.

Despite Piazzetta's thundery tonality, bold shadows and deliberately plebeian people, his affinities in such work are with Watteau who also had so often avoided a 'subject' in the literal sense. Piazzetta's peasants have nothing in common with the dirty sordid peasants of Ceruti; his peasants, if indeed one can call them such, have all the picturesqueness and the 'privateness' of gipsies—and they give the same sense of impermanence.

Pictures like the *Idyll* are rare in Piazzetta's work, but the people in them are virtually the same as those he had postulated as saints and kings in his 'history' pictures where French critics like Cochin had found them so distressingly undigni-fied. It is doubtful if Cochin knew Piazzetta's genre work other than, probably, his 'Peasant' heads; but he at least had no illusions about Piazzetta as a realist. It was a pity, he thought ironically, that Nature, though so beautiful, was not nearly as beautiful as 'the pictures of Tiepolo and Piazzetta'. The age that, with Diderot, preferred Teniers to Watteau could not perhaps be at ease with the fantastic

57. GIAMBATTISTA PIAZZETTA: *An Idyll on the Sea-Shore*. Cologne, Wallraf-Richartz Museum

imaginative genre of Piazzetta, a genre that had exceeded nature and, in fact, no longer tried to be natural.

But genre in the sense of topical comment upon daily life did find a final rather private practitioner, working much more swiftly and satirically than Longhi, in Giambattista Tiepolo's son, Domenico Tiepolo (1727–1804). Domenico's natural talent for genre was for years kept under while he worked as his father's devoted assistant in so many decorative schemes. In those years he had to take his opportunities where he could find them, or invent them. The passage at the left in one of his religious pictures, the *Lot and Abraham* (fig. 58), shows where his real interest lay; in fact he builds up a whole irrelevant genre incident which displays an ability unequalled by any of his contemporaries in its depiction of North Italian country life. He has not Piazzetta's forceful poetry (though his cow is like a borrowing from Piazzetta's cow), but he effortlessly avoids the commonplaceness of Longhi, whom he shames again in his dazzling draughtsmanship. The nearest parallel to the genre-religious treatment here is in the work of the seventeenth-century painter Castiglione, a person much appreciated in eighteenth-century Venice. Domenico suffered, and still suffers, by juxtaposition to a genius, his father. Fastened to those chariot wheels he was forced into regions where he could barely breathe and his art was forced to posture and pastiche in mistaken filial devotion.

It is not very easy to see why Domenico remained confined, unless it was because little patronage was available for the type of work at which he excelled. As assistant he had a hundred uses and he was occasionally rewarded, it would seem, by being given a free hand to insert some lively topicality amid the cloudy imaginative splendours of his father's work. The age looked upon Tiepolo and his sons as *one* painter, a firm in fact, and the very distinctions we now try to draw were concealed beneath a single identity. 'Tiepolo' was all the more versatile, in the eyes of the age, that he could fresco you a mythological scene or a witty piece of contemporary life.

A very few years after the *Lot and Abraham*, the firm received its most balanced commission: to decorate the Valmarana family villa (just outside Vicenza), and the adjoining guest-house. In the villa the vast majority of the frescoes, taken from Homer, Virgil, Tasso and Ariosto, are by Giambattista Tiepolo. But in the guest-house, the *foresteria*, all but one of the seven rooms were given to Domenico, who signed and dated a fresco there 1757. The occasion for this extensive decoration is not, unfortunately, known; it would be tempting to suppose that the marriage of the then owner, Conte Gaetano Valmarana, initiated the scheme. Domenico's frescoes have an enchanting gaiety and wit and freshness, which suggests grateful release from the bondage of being elevated and serious. He proliferates in peasants and pumpkins and meals out of doors, as well as including some scenes of city life—that is, life at Venice.

Never again anywhere else, not even on the walls of the Tiepolo's own villa, did Domenico portray so extensively and romantically life of the time; he did in fact pass out of being observer of genre into being creator of a world as enchanted in its way as his father's. The *Peasants' Meal* (fig. 59) is not just country manners

58. DOMENICO TIEPOLO: *Lot and Abraham*. Rome, Carandini collection

58A. Detail from fig. 57

58B. Detail from fig. 58

59. DOMENICO TIEPOLO: *The Peasants' Meal*. Vicenza, Villa Valmarana

charmingly delineated, but is an almost sentimental pastoral that anticipates while
surpassing nineteenth-century ideas of the rustic. It has only to be compared with
the efforts of Ceruti for Domenico's delight in pleasing to be apparent. His graceful
green and bronze trees and the exquisite strip of fencing are illusionist: beautifully
painted and deceptive cardboard. The peasants are wittily observed, a pregnant
silhouette in the woman at the right, the tall-hatted shape of the man at the table,
and painted in pastel blues and browns and white. Though there is artifice here, it is
not the over-rouged artifice of Boucher's pastorals but the blended sophistication

60. DOMENICO TIEPOLO: *Peasants Reposing*. Vicenza, Villa Valmarana

and naïvety that Mozart gives his peasants; and the world of Domenico's imagining anticipates that of Masetto and Zerlina.

Domenico's power in such scenes is in his control of the artificial element, so that looking carelessly we accept his scenes as of 'real' life. And he remains all the time acutely aware of people and landscape to an extraordinary degree. The *Peasants Reposing* (fig. 60) is a type of pastoral never attempted before, balancing as it does on a razor's edge between naturalism and idealization. It is a fresco of a siesta that will never end: where the trees, half touched by premature autumn, will never lose

their leaves. The pale, drowsy, flat landscape of the Lombard plain, which is suggested, shimmers in the sunlight which has washed the honey-yellow and white
clothes of the elegantly nonchalant peasants into such purity of tone. Domenico
makes marvellous use of his father's lessons in flooding frescoes with light and air.
Both these frescoes are on walls of one quite small room and in both Domenico
dissolves the wall into these light-filled landscapes with their wide expanses of
nearly cloudless sky. Other, less elaborate scenes complete the room; in one
Domenico's favourite device of showing people from the back is used with devastat-
ing effect upon two peasant women in flat hats and high-heeled shoes (fig. 61), the
right-hand of whom, as they set out along the sunlit road, seems already to be
tottering in that way Italian women always do, their shoes being always too small.

Wit and observation drip from Domenico's brush. Freaks of fashionable costume, the trivia of muffs and umbrellas and fans, striped stuffs, absurd silhouettes:
his eye misses none of them and his satire gets mingled with delight at them. The
other rooms of the *foresteria* are full of gaiety, though nothing approaches the
limpid pastoral mood of the room of country scenes. But Venice is there with a
fresco of the masked crowds at the popular diorama, the *Mondo Novo*, and in another with a quack advertising his wares at carnival times; both subjects sound like
those of Longhi, but their brio easily eclipses his pedestrian approach. In another
room, decorated in the Gothic manner, Domenico contrasts winter and summer in
two groups, one aristocratic, the other rustic. At each turn his mind takes effortless
flights of fancy. He could have painted twenty villas like Valmarana, but he was not
required to, unfortunately. Further testimony to his fecund gift for genre is in his
many drawings, private expressions for the most part of his personality, and in a
few oil paintings. Valmarana remained unique, and largely unknown. Goethe penetrated there in 1786; unaware of anyone but 'Tiepolo' he preferred in fact Domenico's frescoes to Giambattista's and he caught the joyful mood of these.

Domenico Tiepolo lived long enough to see not only the rise of a neo-classic style
but its firm establishment. When, after the death of his father at Madrid in 1770, he
returned to Italy it was a return to a colder and more factual world: one actually in
which he was more at home. Only once again, and then not at Venice, did he
undertake a scheme of decoration in his father's manner. Instead, his talent for
topical observation at last found free play, and new subjects for satire. At his own
private villa at Zianigo he frescoed everywhere: on the walls, between windows,
above doors, and some traces of his work remain *in situ*. Animals and birds and the
half-wistful white punchinelli appear, and frescoes of genre—the figures tricked out
in the very latest fashion of the 1790's. Domenico was sixty-four when he dated his
repetition of the 'Mondo Novo' fresco of Valmarana on his own wall. Working so
late in the century, and linked to Spain by his last journey abroad, he inevitably
recalls the fact that Goya had by that time already completed his genre cartoons for

61. DOMENICO TIEPOLO: *Two Peasant Women*. Vicenza, Villa Valmarana

62. DOMENICO TIEPOLO: *A Trio Walking*. Venice, Ca' Rezzonico

so many tapestries, and these subjects are the nearest parallels to Domenico's work. New requirements and new ideas had altered the subjects of Spanish tapestries from heroic and mythological scenes to scenes of daily life in Madrid and in the countryside, just as taste had shifted in Italy.

Domenico remains of the eighteenth century in his uncomplicated belief that people, and the clothes they wear, are funny. His *Trio out for a walk* (fig. 62), which is probably from the very last years of the century, shows him once again indulging in the simple device of seeing his characters from behind. The fresco is from Zianigo, and in it Domenico is painting solely to amuse himself and his family. His three smart yet absurd figures walking off into the eternal Tiepolesque land-scape, accompanied by the servant and dogs, are almost the last Venetian eigh-teenth-century depiction of its people and their world.

The faint light above the background hills is the light of another century and, like the final shot of a film, these figures are advancing into that dawn. Domenico's affection for his own world is impossible to resist; it is already nostalgic, looking back over its shoulder—like the man at the left in the fresco—and full of the feeling of time past, never to be regained.

V

PORTRAIT PAINTING

THE portrait was probably the most popular category of painting throughout eighteenth-century Europe. Yet, when the century was over, and there remained only the thousands of portraits it had produced, these seemed to have
lost even *human* interest. A new generation looked, and found them pompous and
heavy and ridiculous.

And so Coleridge—discussing art as he discussed everything—thought of the
period as decadent and as a good example of decadence he cited Francesco Algarotti's tomb at Pisa, with 'its portraits in periwigs sculptured realistically'. They
alone are enough to damn it, and by the time of Coleridge's comment the periwig
itself has become almost a symbol of a pompous florid style of portrait, whether
sculpted or painted, which a new and easier age found artificial and repellent. And
well before the end of the eighteenth century voices had been raised against the
pomposities of the period; and protests had been made specifically against the
florid artifices of certain portrait painters.

The general trend, and the reaction, are certainly to be found in eighteenth-
century Venice. But the portrait painters in Venice were not on the whole particularly distinguished, nor important, nor—with one exception—were they particularly famous. Outside Venice, they were ignored; nor was there reason to pay them
any attention for they were easily eclipsed by the brilliant variety of great portrait
painters in England and France, and even, to some extent, the rest of Italy. When
Allan Ramsay arrived in Italy quite early in the century it was to Rome that he
chose to go—not Venice—and when he moved from Rome it was to Naples, where
he became Solimena's pupil.

The attitude of Europe is understandable. Whereas Italy was still the true home
of history painting, portrait painting had been superbly well practised outside
Italy during the seventeenth century and the tradition was firmly established. It was
not likely that later Italian painters would contribute importantly to the tradition in
portraiture, and Allan Ramsay's training in Italy with 'modern' painters is an
exceptional case rather than the rule.

But of course Italy remained the home of the Old Masters, and the greatest
contribution made by Venice was that it had been the home of Titian. It is of him
that painters like Reynolds and Wilson speak when in Venice; they do not make
notes about contemporary portrait painters and probably hardly noticed that there
were any. The Venetian portraitists could be said to have worked quite unnoticed and

unapplauded were it not for the extraordinary and immense fame enjoyed through-out Europe by Rosalba Carriera (1675–1757). Rosalba initiated something quite new in portraiture, and it is partly the fault of history that it is now hard for us to share the eighteenth century's enthusiasm. She is perhaps the first 'rococo' artist, and the lightness of her style is welcome among the shadows of the seventeenth century into which she was born. The great tradition of Venetian Renaissance portraiture had been carried on, mechanically but not totally pointlessly, by Domenico Tintoretto in a style that vaguely recalled his father's. His death in 1637 marks the extinction of the real Renaissance tradition; but a shadowy sort of activity continued in the produc-tion, often by anonymous painters, of state portraits and senatorial portraits, dim, dull journeyman work which is hardly connected with art at all but is mere effigy-making. While this was being practised in obscurity at Venice, the example of Titian and Tintoretto and Veronese was exciting great artists from beyond Italy: Velazquez, Rubens, Rembrandt being the greatest. The artistic hegemony had passed entirely from Venice, and very largely from Italy.

Typical in composition, but well above the average aesthetically, is *The Procurator* (fig. 63) of Sebastiano Bombelli (1635–1716); this smoky crimson and scarlet figure is distantly related to Titian, and retains the traditional opulence of Venetian colouring even though it is colour seen through a heavy tenebroso mist. The con-ception, however, is really quite unrelated to the portraits by Titian and Tintoretto which had shown the officials of Venice in moments of private repose, and presented them too with penetrating insight. Such intimate portraits had most often been bust lengths, but now the full length, which Titian for instance had reserved for his very grandest sitters, was used for every senatorial and procuratorial portrait. And in-stead of Titian's combination of intimacy with dignity, as in the *Charles V* at Munich, the new conception emphasized the sitter's importance and distance from the beholder, who was now inspired by feelings of respect and awe. Titian's picture is of a tired old man who is also a monarch, but Bombelli's is the portrait of an official first and last, despite a certain liveliness in the face.

These full-lengths, which were to become so frequent and popular in eighteenth-century Venice, derive in the first place from the big votive paintings of the Renaissance, in which senators and doges solemnly kneel before an altar or a divine personage and in which they personify Venice. Everything in those pictures empha-sized the hieratic: the grave profile and dignified gesture, the rich official clothes, all subduing the personality so that each man becomes only a symbol of the Republic itself.

But in the later work, the divine element has disappeared. The direct personal intervention of the Madonna or the patron saint could not be so firmly guaranteed; the fashion for officialdom and families to be painted enjoying a private vision (of which the last great example is Rubens' votive picture of the Gonzaga family) began

L

63. SEBASTIANO BOMBELLI: *A Procurator*. Venice, Galleria Querini-Stampalia

64. SEBASTIANO BOMBELLI: *The Avogadori Pietro Garzoni and Francesco Benzon.*
Venice, Palazzo Ducale

to dwindle. It is true that during the seventeenth century at Venice, as elsewhere, a sort of semi-votive type of picture continued to be painted for state officials, most often for the 'Avogadori', and examples of such pictures by, for instance, Domenico Tintoretto survive in the depths of the Doges' Palace; but gradually the divine element in them becomes only a slight symbol which the kneeling figures virtually ignore. By the time of Bombelli's double portrait of the *Avogadori Pietro Garzoni and Francesco Benzon* (fig. 64), painted about 1683–84, we have only the undramatic Dove in the sky above the two men, one of whom rather shyly indicates its presence. The picture is frankly a double portrait, a vividly human one in which the celestial appurtenance is barely a distraction; and in other portraits of similar personages by Bombelli even this last faint intrusion is replaced by a plain setting about the figures. People can no longer feel sure of being singled out by heaven. But while the idea still persisted that such heavenly machinery dignified the portrait, a curious solution was arrived at by Francesco Maffei (1600–60) who, though largely active in his native city of Vicenza, also worked at Venice and was influenced by the Venetians. Evolving his own remarkable iconography for such official events as the election of mayors, Maffei conceived full-length portraits in which the personage is wreathed about at times by non-sacred but still moral personifications. The *Glorification of the Podestà Pisani* (fig. 65) is typical of this work, and Pisani stands stiffly encircled by cloudy abstractions like Nobility and Clemency—but he alone is felt as *real*.

After Maffei the last step was to dismiss abstractions of every kind, and the worlds of supernatural and natural are kept apart except occasionally in some allegorical ceiling. There are no portraits of donors introduced into religious pictures in eighteenth-century Venice and no patron saints proffer their namesakes to God or the Virgin. Official portraits are most often full length, and the sitter occupies as much as possible of the picture area, the setting being no more than a loop of tasselled curtain and a fragment of balustrade. The same frontal pose goes on being repeated with hardly any variation, and the official confronts us, one hand clasping his gloves and a thin smile of ambiguous benevolence on his full lips. And their perpetual smiles recall how struck Goethe was by the benevolent aspect of officials in a procession he saw at Venice.

To Rosalba this formal world was quite alien, and undoubtedly one of her gifts in the eyes of her European contemporaries was her intimacy and charm. She first drew attention to a new and graceful renaissance of the arts in Italy. The patrons of Watteau, and Watteau himself, welcomed her for bringing back a beauty which had not been seen since Correggio died; they did not hesitate to compare her with Correggio, and the comparison was not altogether far-fetched.

Rosalba had begun very humbly at Venice before the eighteenth century by designing patterns for lace, that *point de Venise* which formed an export and a source

65. FRANCESCO MAFFEI: *The Glorification of the Podestà Pisani.* Vicenza, Museo Civico

of revenue for the city. It is part of the waning of the Republic that its exports too collapsed, and the lace trade slumped while Rosalba was still quite young. She then took up the painting of snuff boxes whose ivory tops offered scope for decoration, work hardly more remunerative than Renoir's in the Limoges factory; but as with Renoir this early training influenced her style, and decorativeness remained one of her aims in portraiture. Soon she was painting miniatures on ivory ovals separated from the snuff boxes. The soft caressing effect that she sought could in fact be better conveyed in a different medium, pastel, and so Rosalba took up pastel portraiture, perhaps under the influence of Felice Ramelli, a pastel portraitist of the day who was a friend of hers.

By 1705 she was already sufficiently established to be elected a member of the Accademia di S. Luca at Rome. Outside Italy, it was probably the English who first discovered her but it was the French who wooed her. When Pierre Crozat, the collector and amateur, was in Venice in 1715 he met Rosalba and on his return to Paris started that correspondence whose intention, and culmination, was Rosalba's triumphant arrival in Paris five years later. Once there she was fêted by all the most distinguished figures in Parisian artistic circles. But at Venice, during her early career, she did not live in such a very different milieu, close friends with the elder Anton Maria Zanetti, extensively patronized by Joseph Smith, and sister-in-law of Pellegrini who, having been carried off by the Earl of Manchester to England, became virtually her agent in England. One of her sisters had shown an interest in the arts by marrying Pellegrini and another, Giovanna, studied pastel under Rosalba whose work she dutifully but lifelessly copied. Rosalba's household, presided over for long by her mother, was permanently and almost exclusively a studio. The mother was a widow, and the two daughters did not marry; Rosalba's life was one of frightening activity, letter writing and music making alone interrupting her pastel work, and it is all the more pathetic that the blindness of her final years severed her from the only things she had ever done.

Not since Bernini had an Italian artist had such a reception as greeted Rosalba at Paris. During her stay, 1720–21, she kept a *Diario*, less a diary than a terse day-book of whom she saw and whom she drew, but it is a document of almost Proustian social implications, ranging from the very young Louis XV (of whom she executed two pastels) down to inevitable ubiquitous duchesses.

The only disappointment felt was in Rosalba's appearance, for she was plain to the point of ugliness; yet her femininity offered opportunities at least for literary gallantry and even Mariette composed a sonnet in Italian for her where the rose (Rosa) and the dawn (Alba) mingle in insipid imagery. She was made a member of the Académie Royale to whom, once back in Venice, she submitted a reception piece of a Nymph, one of those alluring 'fancy' pieces, blend of the real and the ideal which so titillated the amateurs of her age. In 1730 she was tempted abroad

66. ROSALBA CARRIERA: *Self-Portrait*. Windsor Castle
Reproduced by gracious permission of Her Majesty the Queen

again, this time to Vienna where the Paris success was not eclipsed and where, despite appreciation, the atmosphere was less laudatory.

There is really no evolution in Rosalba's style, and only two types of pastel: portraits and 'fancy' pieces. She had quite a shrewd eye for character and, at least in her self-portraits, was capable of almost savage observation. That late self-portrait which she executed for Joseph Smith (fig. 66) shows that she had observed

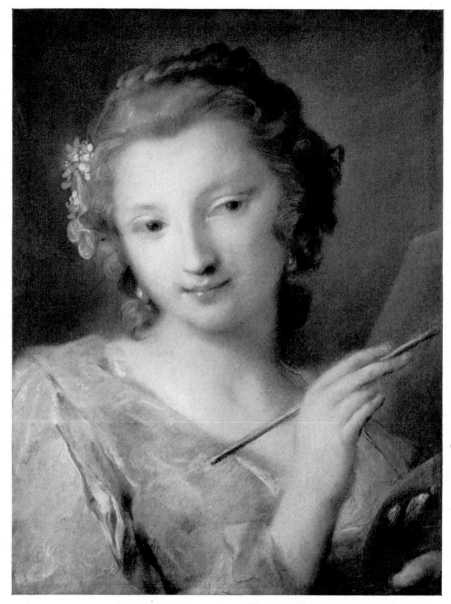

67. ROSALBA CARRIERA: *Allegory of Painting*.
Washington, National Gallery of Art, Samuel H. Kress Collection

herself quite clearly, with none of the softness and charm she liberally distributed to others; and the personality here is tragic, myopic, sober and unromanticized. It is almost too harsh a contrast to her conception of, for example, *The Allegory of Painting* (fig. 67) with her sly seductiveness. We know that Rosalba intended the effect of tragedy in portraits of herself in old age, for in more than one of these she appears

68. ROSALBA CARRIERA: *Horace Walpole*. Wolterton Hall, Lord Walpole collection

as the *Muse of Tragedy*, the only fictitious element a laurel wreath about her sparse grey hair.

For other sitters she contented herself with a good likeness without commenting on the personality. That was not her business, and she made little effort to alter her formula which was to draw a bust-length portrait against a plain background, with only slight variations between a set of stock poses. No doubt the age appreciated the tact she showed in accepting people at their face value and when the occasion called for it she could positively flatter; so that one of her pastels of Louis XV showed the king in noble attitude, 'accompanied by a Victory which seemed to indicate the road to Glory.' In general, however, the medium of pastel provided its own flattery—rather like a peach-coloured mirror—and Mariette forgave Rosalba's incorrect drawing because of the beauty of her colour. Less professional people probably did not express even that mild demur but succumbed to her technique straightaway.

As early as 1719 Rosalba admitted to diverting to Paris an order for six pictures really meant for England. The English, so much more assiduous as tourists than the French, were then already patronizing Rosalba and many visitors brought back portraits of themselves by her. Such lists of her sitters as have survived from after her return from Paris show many more foreigners, named and unnamed, than natives. The great admirers and collectors of her work were no more Venetian than were the admirers and collectors of Canaletto's, and Rosalba's postbag reveals her as besieged by potential patrons in England, Holland, Germany and Austria.

Sometimes the portraits brought back by the English were copied at home by amateur pastellists, and these too in the course of time came to be supposedly by 'Roselby'—as we find her name spelt. Many young men doing the Grand Tour sat to her for a portrait which was also in part a souvenir. A more striking example than most is the portrait of a young man in Venetian masquerade costume, apparently Horace Walpole (fig. 68), which exists in more than one version. The picture has great charm, even if charm does not conceal a sort of epicene silliness. In it Rosalba has pushed her technique to the utmost in delineating the different textures of the furred cloak, the domino's lace, embroidered waistcoat, all of which set off the blooming texture of the flesh. It is rare for her to draw anyone as so obviously a tourist; in many of her portraits in fact it is hard to say whether the sitter was native or visitor. This pastel seems to commemorate an occasion as well as record a likeness; it is easy to imagine the sitter in a colder climate and at a later time explaining what his costume is and why he was wearing it. The fragility of pastel gives rise to its own nostalgia, as de Nerval, poet of pure nostalgia, has not failed to notice in *Sylvie* where two eighteenth-century pastel portraits evoke the 'bon vieux temps' of youth and happiness. In Rosalba's pastel we are reminded how few of those visiting Italy in their youth were ever able to return to Italy later. Nor is this merely a modern reaction; thus, Sir Adam Fergusson of Kilkerran on his return from the Grand Tour ordered from Zuccarelli (then in London) an 'Et ego in Arcadia', anticipating Goethe's use of the phrase in the same connection, suggesting a marvellous experience that is past.

As for the faint suggestion of femininity, Rosalba spread it satisfactorily over her whole art in a way that her period adored. However disappointing she might be as incarnation of woman herself, she did not disappoint taste in the women of her pastels. Apart from portraits, and perhaps in preference to them, there were her 'fancy' subjects, allegories of Art or the Seasons or the Elements, all represented by piquantly sly girls whose conscious allure anticipates the women of Greuze. Like him, Rosalba does not make plain whether these are portraits or imagined beauties; Crozat had a friend M. de Laporte who was on tenterhooks over this very point— he longed to meet, he said, a particular one of these charming people, if indeed the model was from the life. What Rosalba replied to this is not, unfortunately, recorded, but the request alone establishes the atmosphere of gallantry in which her pastels were enjoyed. The *Allegory of Painting* reveals how little different her conception of subject pieces was from her portraiture; the properties of brush and palette matter no more than do elsewhere a bird or a flower in the hand. Eyes were concentrated rather upon the attractive coyness of the expression and the half-shielded interesting disarrangement of linen at the bosom.

The element of trickery in all this only made it more enjoyable. Autumn, a Muse, Virtue, were abstractions rather than realities in any sense; their personification as graceful and compliant girls was a fancy not a serious allegory, and part of the fun was seeing the disguise slip and the personification turn into a woman. Rosalba's ability to understand and satisfy this need was taken solemnly on a very high level. Crozat wrote to thank her for one of her fancy pieces just received at Paris and to say how impressed he had been, incidentally, by seeing the antique sculpture brought back from Italy by Cardinal de Polignac. But, he goes on to say, the pastel she sent is comparable to the finest busts ever made by 'those Greeks': a compliment he was under no obligation to make unless he meant it.

That was in 1732 when Rosalba was internationally famous. Boucher, for example, had hardly appeared on the scene and it was only in the light of the frivolous and lecherous graces of the next few years that Rosalba was to seem insipid. But she had been a pioneer in the style that succeeded in swamping her; pastellists more varied and better equipped arose in France, and even in England, and a whole galaxy of portraitists for ever beyond her emulation. In Venice she worked very privately and the great collection of her pastels was in Dresden where Augustus III assembled quantities; in Venice the most assiduous of her patrons was, once again, Joseph Smith. And at Venice, though she had portrayed Sebastiano Ricci, she does not seem to have been in touch with the famous painters of the new generation. It is another portraitist, not she, of whom we hear that Tiepolo and Piazzetta and Pittoni had begged their likenesses: Bartolomeo Nazari, who had also early painted Canaletto's portrait.

The isolation in which her last years were passed was final. Although Algarotti still wanted work from her for Dresden as late as 1743, her activity was cut short by blindness two years later. An operation temporarily relieved it, but it returned permanently shortly after and she retired into utter melancholy.

Outside Venice she was not forgotten. When Cochin came to Venice at the mid-point of the century he particularly hoped for an interview with her, but it was probably not granted. Some years after her death, her old friend Mariette was preparing an entry about her for his dictionary of painters but lacked the date of her birth. He was in touch with the Venetian architect and scholar, Temanza, who promised to send a copy of the document—but the promise was not quite fulfilled. Temanza repeatedly sent the birth certificate of Rosalba's sister, as Mariette patiently but firmly kept pointing out. And in the end, even the persistence of the Frenchman weakened; he compiled a highly complimentary biography of his friend without the relevant date.

While Rosalba had lived and worked entirely at Venice, apart from her visits to Paris and Vienna, there had been other early eighteenth-century Venetian portrait-ists at work, active chiefly outside Venice. Niccolò Cassana (1659–1714) had lived in London and been patronized by Queen Anne, and his style shows more trace of Kneller's influence than of any of the Venetians'. It has sometimes been said that he was among the first to anticipate the lightness and grace of the new century, but his pictures offer no evidence of this at all. His sitters, in heavy periwigs and plain dark clothes, are solid and dignified and very dull. Cassana's adventure in coming to England and obtaining royal patronage is chiefly interesting in being the prototype for a much grander and more international painter's adventure: that of Amigoni.

Like Cassana not a native of Venice, Amigoni when at Venice painted few por-traits. But in the portrait, as in his other work, he pioneered a graceful rococo atmosphere—an innovation particularly welcome in England at the court of George II. His sitters remain rather stiff and flat and formal, but he attempts to enliven them by playful *putti* who float about with ducal coronets and coats-of-arms; while pale colour schemes of white and yellow and soft blue-grey enhance the gaiety.

Once, in a moment of sympathy, Amigoni created a portrait group of his friend the *castrato* singer Farinelli with Metastasio, Teresa Castellini, another famous singer, and himself (fig. 69), a picture unique at the period and, unfortunately, never to be repeated in Venice. It is an example of relaxed portraiture, as the figures sit informally in the countryside beyond Bologna (seen in the distance). Nobody in Venice was to ask to be shown so intimately, and Amigoni's picture was painted for Farinelli's own villa just outside Bologna where many years later, in 1770, Dr. Burney saw it hanging. Against the felicitous ease of Gainsborough, for example, Amigoni is stilted, yet his picture is all the same a not unsuccessful attempt to show Farinelli and his friends as ordinary beings in a familiar setting, accompanied by flowers and grass and a favourite dog. Nothing so personal was to be painted at Venice, where the emphasis was upon the sitter's rank and position: his detachment

VII. ROSALBA CARRIERA: *Allegory of Painting*.
Washington, National Gallery of Art, Samuel H. Kress Collection

69. JACOPO AMIGONI: *Farinelli with a Group of Friends*. Melbourne, National Gallery of Victoria

from the ordinary world and yet his success in the world. There are to be no favourite animals, no suggestions of personal ease, and, despite all that is so often said of the city's reputation for civilized pleasures, very little of civilized pleasure in the portraits painted.

The intimate close-ups of Rosalba, so many 'snapshots' of her sitters, were not continued by any successor. The tradition of formal portraiture, which Bombelli had carried into the early years of the eighteenth century, survived until the very last years of the Republic, one more piece of ineffectual propaganda. For the official portraits of senators and procurators, even while remaining their private property, were really painted praise of the city itself and its government. The figures themselves have a curious lack of vivacity and vitality, as if drained of energy under the weight of periwig and ceremonial robes. There is a sense of being given the clothes not the man, and such a portrait as that of *Giovanni Querini* (fig. 71) by a pupil of Bombelli, Pietro Uberti (*ca.* 1671–after 1762?), is typical of this work in which there is a frightening airlessness and aridity. Such a picture is half portrait and half heraldic symbol. It is intended to decorate and dignify the room where it hangs; Joseph Smith singled out in his will just such a portrait of the last Doge Cornaro by Uberti (with a portrait by Dahl), bequeathing them to John Udny, his successor as Consul, and remarking 'not improper ornaments, I hope he'll judge, for the house he inhabits'.

The occasion for painting such work was usually an official event such as election to some office, and it was customary for the portrait to be engraved at the same time. In many cases too the actual portrait was set up on exhibition on the day of the subject's solemn entry into his office. This was the custom for Patriarchs and Procurators, and when Francesco Correr was elected Patriarch he had three portraits of himself put on exhibition, each showing him in a different costume.

With such demands there came, inevitably, supply. Some painters specialized in official work of this kind, and the family of Nazari established themselves almost as 'court' painters, so many commissions for state and semi-state portraits did they execute. Bartolomeo Nazari (1699–1763) was not a native of Venice but of Bergamo, and once again is an example of a portrait painter not trained at Venice. Records of what he painted have survived rather better than the pictures themselves, but his official work conformed to the accepted current style and it was in fact he whom the Patriarch Correr had chosen to paint the three portraits of himself. Nazari was a livelier artist than Uberti, and his pictures—unlike Uberti's—have shaken off totally the shadowy mists of tenebrism; and he was clearly a reliable sort of person to produce a perfectly adequate likeness, exactly the type of Royal Academician whose portrait of the local Mayor could never give offence.

Nazari was actually capable of greater informality than his usual patrons demanded. He was patronized more than once by the English, and his relaxed con-

70. BARTOLOMEO NAZARI: *Lord Boyne with a Group of Friends.* Castle Howard, George Howard collection

71. PIETRO UBERTI: *Giovanni Querini*. Venice, Galleria Querini-Stampalia

72. NAZARIO NAZARI: *Andrea Tron*. London, National Gallery

versation piece of *Lord Boyne and friends* (fig. 70), where the group sit talking in Lord Boyne's cabin, is a commonplace of English painting without parallel in Italian painting of the same date. It took very different patrons to produce such a very different picture as this. Equally out of the ordinary was an equestrian portrait of Marshal Schulenburg, that patron of Canaletto and Carlevaris, which Nazari is recorded as having painted—though the horse was not his work. One or two vague rumours reach us of other equestrian portraits painted at the period, but hardly anything has survived to substantiate these or suggest what style of picture they were. It is difficult to say if Gradenigo has made a mistake, or if his note that Tiepolo had received a commission from George II to paint an equestrian portrait of Frederick the Great does record a remarkably unique fact; if the latter, it is unlikely that the commission ever resulted in a picture and perhaps with the subsequent death of George II the matter was dropped. Such equestrian portraits as were painted were probably not great life-size pieces, but small semi-genre work of the type produced once or twice by Pietro Longhi.

The more conservative tradition was inherited and continued by Bartolomeo's son, Nazario Nazari (1724–after 1793), who in at least one portrait has summed up finally the concept of the Venetian aristocrat as servant of the State: *Andrea Tron* (fig. 72). There might seem at first glance little difference between Uberti's portrait of some fifty years earlier and this picture, painted about 1770. But apart from Nazari's more vivid presentation, there is also a more vivid sense of what may be called propaganda. The time had not yet come when David was to paint Napoleon working late in his study, while the candles gutter and the rest of France is asleep. Yet the intention behind this portrait is rather similar, with its complete evocation of an actual rococo-panelled room, its litter of documents and ink wells and quill pens, and the imposing figure with a face of shrivelled benevolence who seems to occupy the whole space. Tron is not shown as Procurator, but he had as senator and ambassador already been long in service of the State and here he discreetly exudes that air of power which won for him the nickname of *El Paron*, the patron who was also an *eminence grise*. His power is blended with that of the Republic, and official-dom is as clearly revealed by his wig (out of date in ordinary life of the period) as a judge's wig reveals it to-day. The spectator is reminded of what the archaic robes emphasize yet more, that Venice is here: busy and autocratically benevolent, cease-lessly active and always dignified. The carefully observed interior is all part of the scene, very different from Uberti's vacuous settings, and the detail of the littered documents plays its part just as those documents did which Fox, when sitting to Reynolds, asked to have shown beside him marked with titles of Bills he had initiated in Parliament.

The grand manner of Venetian portraiture could achieve nothing finer than *Andrea Tron*, and the whole style collapsed with the collapse of the Republic it celebrated. But there did exist one painter capable of loosening the tradition while it lasted, without quite departing from it. Alessandro Longhi (1733–1813), son of Pietro Longhi, possessed too lively an eye for the idiosyncratic in individuals to submerge it in conventional portraiture. In his hands something could yet be made of the portrait as a piece of intimate and human furniture and in this idea of the portrait as *genre* he had as predecessor his father. Their artistic relationship is still in a muddle, for it seems as if Alessandro's portraits began after a while to influence Pietro. However, Pietro's portraits are few and not particularly exciting. He executed on a small scale one or two family groups, which are blended *genre* and portraiture, and there are also acceptably by him a few rather flat single portraits. A puzzling point about these is whether, and how, they can have influenced Reynolds who was only once and very briefly in Venice, in 1752, and who returned to England to paint portraits which are said by scholars to show Longhi's influence. There can be no doubt of the 'Venetian' quality of such a portrait as Reynolds' *Lord Cathcart* (fig. 73), painted in London a year or two after his return. There is nothing in Pietro Longhi really at all like this; but the manner anticipates Alessandro, who was only nineteen when Reynolds visited Venice. Both painters have gone back to the tradition of the earlier Venetian School and thus they achieve a similarity.

Alessandro was actually trained under Giuseppe Nogari (*ca.* 1700–63), a painter who has only recently been given any coherent artistic personality. Nogari's portraits were competent as far as the head; for anything else, said Tessin, one should go to another painter. As well as portraits, Nogari painted in the *genre* way fanciful peasant heads vaguely Dutch or Flemish in character, watered down pastiches often of Rembrandt. There was a taste for such work in eighteenth-century Venice, and perhaps it helped Alessandro Longhi to flavour his work with a sort of gauche realism more Northern than Italian. While Reynolds was to progress beyond *Lord Cathcart* to a much grander manner and was to recognize the sitter's wish to have his character ennobled, Longhi was going to emphasize the quality and trade of his sitters with determined prosaicism.

Although by no means a good draughtsman, he had ability in the actual handling of paint and a sense of the aesthetic quality of the medium which relates him to Bombelli and back to the great sixteenth-century Venetians themselves. Unlike all his Venetian contemporaries, Alessandro Longhi uses oil paint thickly and creamily, not dissipating it into pale mists of colour but achieving dark, rich, opulent tones. When he exhibited the portrait of an innkeeper on S. Roch's day, 1760, critics immediately recognized a new and different talent. The picture was painted, so it seemed to Gradenigo, *con nuova maniera,* and even the choice of sitter, perhaps, had its novelty. One saw immediately that it was an innkeeper, for the accessories in the portrait, Gradenigo remarked, made clear the profession; and the innkeeper was shown with a knife in one hand, just about to carve a joint.

73. SIR JOSHUA REYNOLDS: *Lord Cathcart*. Sandridge, Lord Cathcart collection

Gasparo Gozzi, then editing his newspaper the *Gazzetta Veneta*, was also struck by Alessandro's *Innkeeper*, and was led by it to remark that there is more than one type of beauty in Nature: his sympathy going out to the 'reality' of Alessandro's work as it went out to Pietro Longhi's 'reality'. Both painters, is the implication, paint what they see rather than what they imagine. Alessandro does not paint a scene, of course, but a person; his people are not shown mingling in society, but occupying their place in society: as innkeeper, writer, cleric,

74. ALESSANDRO LONGHI: *Carlo Goldoni*. Venice, Museo Correr

or whatever it may be. To this extent, the individual is less important than his profession.

It is difficult, if not impossible, to avoid linking Longhi's intentions with the ideal of the portrait as expressed at almost the same time by Diderot. He had been horrified by La Tour's portrait of Rousseau with its combed and powdered appearance in place of the negligent and untidy figure of fact. Instead of portraits where reality is obscured by wigs and fine clothes, he asked for the moment of truth. And he tells the anecdote of the smith whose son asked that his father be painted in his ordinary clothes, with his apron and spectacles, perhaps sharpening or testing a steel blade. What was painted was a beautiful portrait of his father in a fine suit, elegantly holding a snuff box. Ah, exclaimed the young man when he saw it, it's valueless: I asked for my everyday father and here is my Sunday father, *mon père des dimanches.*

It is not surprising therefore that male sitters far outnumber female in Venetian portraits of the period, for the age conceived women's place in society as much more restricted. No woman in Venice, it appears, was ever painted in a large full-length portrait. Still less, one may add, are there any of those gallant female portraits, poised on the edge of pornography, which occupied the time of so many French artists of the period. And there is a certain justness in the fact that Alessandro Longhi never portrayed tourists or visitors, for he could know nothing about them. It does not appear that he ever worked outside Venice; he was chiefly the painter of Venetians, not seen in carnival masks or in official robes but seen as personalities and even friends.

His portrait therefore of Goldoni (fig. 74) has an additional aptness in uniting painter and sitter, for as well as being friends, their ideas had something in common. Neither of course is a revolutionary; hardly anybody in Venice at the time was. But both have a certain feeling for personality and Alessandro is a much more convincing parallel to Goldoni in painting than the usual parallel of Pietro Longhi. Something of Alessandro's interest in human nature is conveyed by his publication in 1762 of a group of biographies of important contemporary Venetian artists, each life illustrated with a portrait engraving by him. And at a later date we hear of him employed in re-creating personality, given the task of painting for the newly founded Academy portraits of the great painters of Renaissance Venice. Alessandro never possessed a part of Goldoni's talents, but he can claim some affinity with the writer who said: 'rien ne m'intéresse davantage que l'analyse du cœur humain.'

His *Goldoni* has a spontaneous and penetrating air, even while negligently charming. There is nothing pompous in the portrait, but one cannot fail to take the hint that here is a writer. Like the innkeeper of a year or two before, Goldoni has his professional accoutrements scattered around him. He himself stands with a book, dressed in ordinary clothes, his features carefully and almost mischievously observed. Nothing could well be less rococo. No *putto* brings his inkwell or offers him a pen, and instead his sidelong glance of shrewdness seems to cross with the painter's glance as the two of them create a climate of scrutiny too cold for *putti* to inhabit. The thickly applied paint with its creamy impasto is at work too in building up a real image, clotted like lace to indicate the lace cravat and thickly rich on the waistcoat with the thickness of brocade. Rosalba would have used her medium to enhance Goldoni, but Longhi uses his to explore the reality of Goldoni.

75. ALESSANDRO LONGHI: *A Prelate.* Venice, Private collection

The picture must be comparatively youthful work, for Goldoni quitted Venice in
1762 never to return. In the Venice he left, stirrings towards a new and better state of
affairs had already begun, but like so much in eighteenth-century Venice they came
to nothing. Nevertheless, it is hard to believe that the new ideas of humanity which
were seeping in—even into Venice—did not play some part in Alessandro Longhi's
attitude to portraiture. Alessandro was to live long enough to see the fall of the

76. ALESSANDRO LONGHI: *Jacopo Gradenigo*. Padua, Museo Civico

77. THOMAS GAINSBOROUGH: *Lord Howe*. London, Earl Howe collection

Republic, to see Napoleon and the French domination. Meanwhile, he painted in a world which was losing all its old assurance, a world rattled by the opinions of those whose books it banned, Rousseau, Diderot and Voltaire among them. Nowhere else, Rousseau thought, showed better than the Venetian Republic that though man is born free he is everywhere in chains. Even Venice could not check Rousseau's influence, and the different weapons of humanity, satire, scrutiny, scorn, were sharpened for attack on the State and the Church, both of which had failed mankind.

Longhi's *Prelate* (fig. 75) is painted with as much frankness as his portrait of Goldoni, but the air of mild mischief there has here become almost malice. It is a portrait Flaubert would have enjoyed. Amid the priestly trappings, the face of peasant *bonhomie* has an expression of uncertainty: a doubt as to whether the dignified pose has not toppled, along with the sitter, into ludicrousness. Longhi has not the temper for satire, any more than had his father; but he paints here with a broad candour that makes one smile, even while he avoids caricature. There is, once again, a genuine sense of personality.

Indeed, Longhi could not perhaps mute his sense of such things even when it would have been discreet to do so. A much later picture, probably of about 1780 or so, is the Venetian naval official *Jacopo Gradenigo* (fig. 76), the design of which is the traditional type used by 'official' portraitists. Longhi's feeling for sumptuous colouring comes out in the gold-embroidered red robes, and the whole picture has an inflated swagger pricked by something indefinable into absurdity. Satiric intent has been suggested to explain the rather ambiguous appearance of Gradenigo, but that is already suggesting too much. It is quite true that the sitter seems to have affinity with some of Goya's portraits, perhaps because of the bland vacuity he has in common with the subjects of those. And one senses the impracticality of the sitter not only as a sailor but as a human being. A piquant contrast is obtained if he is compared with a real seaman painted some fifteen years earlier by Gainsborough, the superbly nonchalant *Lord Howe* (fig. 77). No comment is needed to underline the difference between these two full-length portraits from two eighteenth-century climates. After Lord Howe's gracefully relaxed and capable air, Gradenigo seems only a powdered periwig and some unnautical clothes, a pompous pageant figure proclaiming his outdatedness and his fitness for destruction. In the age of Louis XIV he would have been a trifle overblown and opulent, but in the very late eighteenth century he is a smiling anachronism: one of those portraits in a periwig from which Coleridge and Diderot would have recoiled.

Inevitably Venice evolved only after the rest of Europe evolved, but in the end it too changed its taste and ideals. The coming of the nineteenth century meant a new shift in portraiture and in face painting of every kind. The Venetian portrait painters had been so attached to the reality of the face as it is seen: as a mere likeness. More highflown ideals reigned in the neo-classic period; the faces nature gave us, tricked out in the fashion of the moment, looked sadly prosaic when, for instance, Canova was alive to sculpt a nobler face, or ennoble an ordinary one.

As a sign of the close of the eighteenth-century Venetian portrait world, and as an expression of new devotion to the ideal, Byron's rhapsody before Canova's bust of Helen is not irrelevant. At Contessa Albrizzi's in Venice he saw it often and admired it more; classically calm and ideally beautiful, it raised new standards and new aesthetic problems for an age turning resolutely from the pastels of Rosalba or the portraits of Alessandro Longhi:

> In this beloved marble view
>   Above the works and thoughts of Man,
> What nature *could*, but *would not*, do,
>   And beauty and Canova *can*!

VI

THE PRESIDING GENIUS: GIAMBATTISTA TIEPOLO

AT her death in July 1752 Tiepolo's sister Eugenia bequeathed him nothing. She explains why in her will: because he had so much already. However, she does go on to say that he may have one thing, if he wishes: the pair of portrait engravings of their parents.

There are few other sidelights on Tiepolo's private life, and even this slight one has a certain vivid value. While there may be something of the eternal spinster sister in Eugenia Tiepolo's reference to her brother's prosperity, she gives us a brief glimpse into their family background with parents who were themselves prosperous enough and of sufficient social standing to have their likenesses recorded. And she pays tribute in her way to the colossal success of Tiepolo, actually busy at Würzburg on one of his greatest commissions when she died.

Success is certainly one keynote to Tiepolo's life. From the moment he appeared, as a very young man, on the artistic scene at Venice until his arrival in Madrid nearly fifty years later, he enjoyed fame, health, considerable wealth, and preserved intact his gift of brilliant virtuosity. Seldom ill and never idle, he was the greatest decorative painter of eighteenth-century Europe as well as its most able craftsman. Vast fresco schemes or large altarpieces were undertaken by him as easily as small canvases, drawings, etchings; the sheer bulk of his work in all those media is terrifying to contemplate and assess. There was no artistic aspect of the period at Venice left untouched by him: history pictures, genre in the shape of some caricatures, landscape drawings, even one or two portraits. It is true that he never painted view pictures, but his influence was felt by his brother-in-law, Francesco Guardi, and he at least collected some pictures by Canaletto.

Nevertheless, living and working over such a large part of the century, Tiepolo was inevitably faced with shifting taste. In the active period of his life—from about 1716 to his death in 1770—he never managed to establish a reputation in England, nor was he much esteemed in France. And the Italy of that long period underwent changes which gradually obscured Tiepolo's merit and caused him to meet with open hostility. Summoned to fresco the Royal Palace at Madrid, where he arrived in 1762, Tiepolo asked afterwards to remain in Spain and apparently preferred that life to returning to Venice. Even at the height of his success he was not in demand throughout Italy, but only in the North. Excepting the special circumstances of his Spanish journey, we can say that the kingdom he ruled was a Northern one, extend-

VIII. GIAMBATTISTA TIEPOLO: *The Trinity appearing to S. Clement* (?).
London, National Gallery

ing from Lombardy and the Veneto into Bavaria, and touching also the far Northern courts of Sweden and Russia. This is really more limited a field of activity than that of lesser people like Pellegrini and Amigoni. It omitted Paris, Rome, and London.

But those three capitals were the centres of the new ideas that heralded Tiepolo's neglect and disgrace. Paris possessed in Boucher a contemporary decorative painter who himself began to receive abuse by the very early 1760's; Rome was to become the home of Winckelmann and of Mengs; London was to see a dogma of aesthetics laid down in the *Discourses* of Reynolds where Tiepolo's name is never mentioned. Winckelmann mentioned Tiepolo, but only to compare him scornfully with Mengs: Tiepolo, he says, paints more in a day than Mengs in a week, but the former's work once seen is forgotten whereas the work of Mengs is fixed forever in the memory. And before the end of the eighteenth century Italian critics were already discussing Tiepolo and the modern Venetian school in much the same terms.

It is against that shifting background of taste that Tiepolo's achievement must be seen. The denigration that he endured, especially that his reputation endured, continued well into the nineteenth century and is probably still with us to-day to some extent. There are reasons both good and bad for this. The most understandable is the fact that all Tiepolo's great work remains *in situ* in the churches and palaces of his artistic kingdom and must be seen to be appreciated; even the best photographs give poor indications of its settings and ambience. The least understandable of the prejudices against Tiepolo is against his virtuoso speed, something that his contemporaries enjoyed in the very different art of Metastasio ('I Pittori presti sono come i Poeti all' improviso,' a contemporary remarked) and were to enjoy in the music of Mozart.

Like Metastasio and Mozart, Tiepolo was brilliantly precocious. Born at Venice in the spring of 1696, he must have been early apprenticed as an artist. From the first he was a legend and is marked out as the genius which—almost surprisingly— he became. In so many ways Tiepolo is the last of Renaissance painters and his precocity seems to belong in the Renaissance; his exhibiting with great success a picture at S. Rocco when only twenty, is the sort of story Vasari would have loved and Vasari would have appreciated, too, Tiepolo's effortless facility.

It is part of the legend that this picture, a *Crossing of the Red Sea*, is lost, disappears in fact from history after a single mention at the period. Something of its style can be inferred, since a still earlier painting by Tiepolo has survived, and a number of pictures have survived by his first master Gregorio Lazzarini (1665– 1730). Indeed, Lazzarini more than once painted the same subject as the lost work, and the dramatic Old Testament episode had already been the subject of a cantata performed at San Giorgio Maggiore at Venice in 1682. More relevant, probably, was the existence of Renaissance treatment of the subject in the well-known and very large woodcut based on Titian. And the subject's overtones of grand manner

N

continue into the nineteenth century; it was the very episode chosen by Marcel in Murger's 'Vie de Bohème' for the picture he never finishes.

Lazzarini is yet one more of those awkward figures straddled between two centuries and two styles; his *Charity of S. Lorenzo Giustinian* (fig. 78), painted for San Pietro in Castello, and still *in situ*, shows a certain decorative gift and feeling for colour. His studio was situated in the parish of San Pietro, where the Tiepolo family also lived; apart from proximity, however, he offered Tiepolo some training in decorative painting and was himself popular and famous, much patronized by the aristocracy and still in vogue after his death. Thus Consul Smith, who seldom if ever patronized Tiepolo, possessed paintings by Lazzarini. John Strange recognized in him 'the first modern painter of the Venetian School, who, from that dark unpleasant manner, before used, changed his stile to the lively and graceful'. That testimony (of 1789) is early tribute to his importance at the period.

The Tiepolo family seems to have had its own patrons among the aristocracy. Although merely a plain citizen Domenico Tiepolo, the painter's father, was able to call on noble families for godparents to his children. Domenico died when Tiepolo was barely a year old, but perhaps his connections were later of use. While still in his early twenties the painter is recorded as 'curator' of the then Doge's art treasures, as well as working for him as an artist himself. And he was soon employed by other noble Venetians.

Quite early Tiepolo apparently broke away from Lazzarini, having learnt no doubt all the older mediocre man could teach him. Instead, Alessandro Longhi records, he derived from study of Veronese a 'maniera Paolesca': very different from the sombre and timid manner of Lazzarini. And it was exactly a 'maniera Paolesca' of course that Sebastiano Ricci had formed. In a Venice where Ricci and his pupils had already painted canvases in this new style, Tiepolo was growing up. Yet his early pictures contain no hints that he had looked at Ricci's work at all: the first picture we know of, the *Sacrifice of Isaac* (fig. 79) in the Ospedaletto, is in the very style that Ricci was making redundant. Painted about 1716, this decoration for a spandrel shows Tiepolo far from out of sympathy with seventeenth-century ideals. It suggests that Piazzetta, of all painters then living, was the one who most interested and influenced him. Nothing suggests a great decorator or even a particularly gifted artist, and Tiepolo's contemporaries must be congratulated on their acuteness in hailing this young painter.

Quite a few of Tiepolo's other early pictures show him apeing the style of the un-rococo painters of the period, and show as here the almost brutally prosaic way he then treated his subject matter. It took time for his own true manner to evolve; when it did it was different both from the peculiar 'reality' of Piazzetta and from Ricci's plagiaristic pseudo-Veronese style. Nor was Tiepolo to be in any way a 'learned' painter. In approaching historical and religious subjects with a jaunty

78. GREGORIO LAZZARINI: *The Charity of S. Lorenzo Giustinian.* Venice, S. Pietro in Castello

79. GIAMBATTISTA TIEPOLO: *The Sacrifice of Isaac* (detail). Venice, Ospedaletto

romantic air he was in the best tradition of Venetian painting which had always been unlearned.

One handicap to the evolution of Tiepolo's own style was the fact that oil painting never suited him as well as fresco. Perhaps he never properly mastered the technique of oil paint, and it remains true of all his work in the medium that the more he 'finishes' a picture the heavier it becomes. His sureness of touch and instinctive draughtsmanship show at their best in frescoes where the paint must be laid directly onto the wet plaster, and retouching is virtually impossible. Here, as in his drawings, the light-coloured background was utilized to give light and space; it shines through the washes of colour and floods the whole composition with liquid air. No doubt to achieve a similar effect, Tiepolo seems usually to have laid in a pale buff ground over his canvases before painting in oils; but a luminous effect is not properly achieved by this, and in large elaborate pictures little of the ground shows through under heavy layers of worked paint.

The division between frescoes and oil paintings extends beyond technique. Whereas frescoes were quite frankly decorative, oil paintings had often to be of sterner or more humble subjects. Again and again we find Tiepolo producing an air-filled ceiling fresco, all shimmering colour and grace, while almost contemporaneously he is labouring at some altarpiece which has to be in a vein of more solid realism. Only gradually did he manage to invest his oil paintings with something of his frescoes' grace, and at last forget the seventeenth-century style training of his youth.

The connoisseurs who applauded him while still a young man indicated, even if they did not quite realize, his suitability as fresco painter. A connoisseur like Vincenzo da Canal appreciated in Tiepolo a manner that was 'resolute and rapid' and a nature 'all spirit and fire'. Tiepolo is by that time (1732) one more example of the new tendencies; he has become rococo. By that time too he had given the most sustained proof of his abilities outside Venice. It was at Udine that he first was given an opportunity to carry out the fresco decorations of a whole room.

The archbishop of Udine, member of the noble Venetian family of the Dolfin, summoned Tiepolo there in 1726 and he was given a commission for some frescoes in a chapel of the cathedral. Already in the documents for these Tiepolo is particularized as 'celebrated'; by the time da Canal writes of him he has become 'most celebrated'. There can hardly be much progression of fame beyond this point. Tiepolo's fame was in fact so taken for granted in the Venice of his day that few people bothered to write down much about him; we are left in the paradoxical position of knowing how famous he was, without having much information about him personally.

Like nearly everything he did, the cathedral frescoes at Udine were a success. The archbishop then employed him on decorating a gallery of the archiepiscopal palace, a narrow, high but well-lit room. The theme for this was taken from the Book of Genesis and is concerned with Abraham and his descendants: a solemn theme, full of anticipations of the New Testament. Whether Tiepolo chose the plan, or whether it was drawn up by some pet cleric of the archbishop's (or by the archbishop himself), the result was rather less solemn than might have been expected. The decoration certainly has a dash of piety to suit its location, but it is gay to the point of flippancy and the Bible seems to have been utilized as might a good book of fairy stories.

The gloomy ponderous effects of Tiepolo's early canvases are banished and replaced by a shimmering series of tableaux full of wit and elegance. Biblical personages are dressed in a romantic version of sixteenth-century costume, borrowed in bits from Veronese, and set in airy landscapes framed by simply painted architecture. Like large pictures the frescoes are painted down the longest unbroken wall and clearly lit by the windows opposite; their first effect is of colour rather than of design, colour such as had not been conceived by any Venetian for at least 150 years. The wall is dazzling in its greens and whites and pale yellows and mauves, and the colour alone prepares the onlooker for the enchanted treatment of the elevated theme.

For in this early commission Tiepolo was faced by a problem that faced all the decorative painters of the century, and which he alone triumphantly solved. The most commonly required themes—whether drawn from religion or history—could no longer be dealt with in a straightforward way; in an age of rational scepticism some method was needed to make many of the stories acceptable even as decoration. Other painters could be more frankly frivolous; many others were 'learned' and pompous. But Tiepolo alone induced credibility: not in the story, but in the world he imagined for the story. That is one of his greatest superiorities over Sebastiano Ricci. The boldness of his imagination shows itself already at Udine. Not only does he invent an annunciation not in the Bible, the *Angel appearing to Sarah* (fig. 80), but he treats the scene in a spirit of sophisticated enchantment. Sarah is clad in a costume exotic to eighteenth-century eyes—a Renaissance dress and ruff—but Biblical indications of her age are observed by leaving her only two teeth and a multiplicity of wrinkles; she kneels in a picturesquely tumble-down workman's shack hung with a piece of rope, some rag and a flask, and some blue convolvulus twine about the base of a tall tree. To her appears the elegantly posed angel in a Renaissance patterned robe hitched up to reveal a bare elegant leg. In the background is a mountainous North Italian landscape which may even be meant for the countryside round Udine.

This mixture of nature observed and the Renaissance recreated is bold enough to compel us to accept its validity, regardless of what it illustrates. It is not so much doctrine in decorative terms, as a scene from which doctrine has receded. The impression conveyed is not of solemnity, still less of reality. Tiepolo has no idea— still less any interest in—how the incident actually occurred in Biblical times. His theme is of a mortal honoured by a visit from an immortal, set in a transfigured countryside part Italy and part the landscape of imagination. This actual fresco was chosen by E. J. Dent as a parallel to the juxtaposition of serious and grotesque in Alessandro Scarlatti's operas; and Sarah suggested to him the same type of comic old woman who keeps appearing in these.

In another fresco, the *Angels appearing to Abraham* (fig. 81), the lulling incantation is so strong that the angels seem part of a hallucination or a dream: they are born like a mirage out of the bare dry landscape where Abraham kneels rapt. The Bible did not guide Tiepolo (at least, not intentionally) to this view of natural and supernatural. His own taste was always for a moment of awe: the magic moment when the heavens open and celestial beings appear. And the frescoes at Udine are really closer in feeling to *The Tempest* than to anything overtly religious.

Whereas these two scenes are magical but undramatic, the version on the ceiling of the *Sacrifice of Isaac* (fig. 82) is a drama which prepares the way for Tiepolo's later treatment of such moments of arrested sacrifice. It is in a very different mood from the Ospedaletto version (fig. 79) that the fresco here is conceived. Instead of the intimate and desperate group of Abraham advancing the knife and Isaac fainting

80. GIAMBATTISTA TIEPOLO: *The Angel appearing to Sarah*. Udine, Archbishop's Palace

81. GIAMBATTISTA TIEPOLO: *The Angels appearing to Abraham.* Udine, Archbishop's Palace

82. GIAMBATTISTA TIEPOLO: *The Sacrifice of Isaac*. Udine, Archbishop's Palace

over the faggots, we are given a *gamin* Isaac sun-bathing in the sudden rays of divine light and a magnificently posed Abraham who is early checked by the angel's arrival. The whole scene is set on a bare mountain peak against a vast expanse of cloudy sky; the composition is a tall dramatically tilted triangle, its apex the source of the light which has suddenly split open the sky. Like a god from a machine, the angel whirls down so fast that his draperies fly out in a mushroom round his waist, and he comes borne by a spiral of smoky cumulus cloud.

In some sense 'reality' may be said to be further away in this later version of the scene. But in its place we are given a moment of pure theatre: intervention by God averts a human tragedy. The ceiling becomes the site of a cloudy cosmic drama. Tiepolo has wonderfully conveyed a sense of Abraham and Isaac as the sole inhabitants of their world; Isaac is doomed; and then the tragic moment passes with the shafts of light cutting darkness and the angel's appearance. Before such scenes the

83. GIAMBATTISTA TIEPOLO: *The Angels appearing to Abraham*. Venice, Scuola S. Rocco

eighteenth-century spectator certainly involved himself emotionally. Of a *Sacrifice of Iphigenia*—the classical counterpart of the Isaac story—the Comte de Caylus said that the spectator should not be struck before having shed tears.

'Theatre' is adumbrated in this fresco at Udine. A few years later, still outside Venice, Tiepolo expressed more maturely his sense of theatre in a fresco series of scenes from Scipio's life. In his altarpieces he was still conscious of the seventeenth century, even while showing some awareness of Ricci. His *Abraham and the Angels* (fig. 83) in the Scuola di San Rocco at Venice, painted about 1732, shows him returning to a sort of 'reality' very different from the dreamy air of the Udine version of the subject, and reveals how far apart he was still keeping his personality in oil paintings from that in his frescoes.

In 1731 two important commissions had taken Tiepolo to Milan. The first was a series of ceilings for Palazzo Archinto, destroyed totally in 1943. Because of that commission, he writes to Conte Casati, he cannot yet undertake the Conte's scheme; but with his usual speed he soon had the Palazzo Archinto frescoes completed and could turn to the *Story of Scipio* frescoes for Palazzo Casati-Dugnani. They too were completed in 1731.

Less witty and dashing than the Udine frescoes, these scenes are serious and elevated. The curtain rises on rococo drama and it is, once again, opera. The subject was planned no doubt as yet one more favourable aspect of rulers—in a century that was becoming increasingly sceptical of rulers. It would be a change, Cochin wrote some twenty years later, to glorify a monarch not through battle pictures but through pictures of royal mercy and generosity taken from history. And the theme of the Palazzo Dugnani frescoes was stated in general allegorical terms on the ceiling with a positive *Triumph of Magnanimity*, while the walls are frescoed with episodes which illustrate the theme in detail. The decoration was thus intended to form a coherent scheme, and in fact the century was usually as careful as here to plan its decorations in units which make up a single theme or story.

And, as here, the ceiling usually becomes by a convenient convention the sky. Heaven is needed, but it is more often a secular and moral heaven where personifications of Nobility and Clemency and Magnanimity triumph bloodlessly and totally over their opposing vices. Just as in the votive portrait religious visions are replaced by moral visions—heroes borne to heaven by their virtues—so here history is interpreted in terms of morality. The triumphs of virtue over vice which are illustrated on so many ceilings of the period are almost like the medieval Psychomachia—the virtues and vices at war in the soul—and they are a sharp reminder of the period's preoccupation with the problem of being good without necessarily believing in God.

In one way of course such triumphs are truisms. But the age of Johnson never despised a sonorous commonplace, as its tombstones bear witness. A foundation of morality was needed to make art acceptable. When in 1753 there was a project for an Academy of Art at Glasgow, the prospectus stated succinctly the age's belief: 'Nothing is grand and sublime but what is highly moral. The fine Arts can never rise to their highest perfection, but when they aim at the moral perfection of Mankind.'

Like the other Venetian history painters, Tiepolo was not as serious as this. He observed the grandiloquent conventions, but he did not believe in them one might

84. GIAMBATTISTA TIEPOLO: *Sophonisba receiving the Poison*. Milan, Palazzo Dugnani

guess. Hence the criticism of him by people like Winckelmann was partly justified, granting their canon of aesthetics. When Reynolds wrote that the Venetian painters were not 'wholly serious' he might have singled out Tiepolo, though he was really thinking chiefly of Veronese. At Palazzo Dugnani Tiepolo demonstrates, for the first time on a grand scale, how he reconciles the 'moral' with decorative needs.

    Three frescoes illustrate what the ceiling states more generally: Scipio is continent at the fall of New Carthage (the scene that Ricci had already treated (fig. 5) and which remained so popular); Scipio releases a prisoner; and, a variation from Roman virtue, Sophonisba the Carthaginian receiving the poison sent by her husband which will grant her death rather than dishonour (fig. 84). Each scene is set in a painted architectural *œil de bœuf* framework very different from Tiepolo's later manipulation of the painted architecture to enhance the composition; here it serves merely as proscenium and the eye passes on from it straightaway to what is happening beyond.

85. GIOVANNI ANTONIO PELLEGRINI: *Sophonisba receiving the Poison*. Schleissheim, Schloss

In the *Sophonisba*, everything is concentrated upon the heroine herself, and not even damage to her has spoilt the effect. The organization of the scene inevitably suggests the opera of the period; Sophonisba is the soprano, the 'star', and the people about her are no more than 'mutes or audience to this act'. Like the chorus of an opera they react without interfering, and nothing distracts attention from the heroine. As the poison arrives she reaches out for it heroically, while consternation seizes her court. It is a moment of drama certainly, but poignant rather than horrific. The deaths and gruesome agonies which had so often been the subjects of seventeenth-century pictures are replaced in the eighteenth century by more affecting scenes; Tiepolo shows us the sort of dramatic moment that Racine could have approved of and it was the French classical tragedy convention that opera had adopted. Needless to say, Tiepolo bothers no more than would an opera with Carthaginian costume and scenery; a mixture of Veronese and fantasy-Oriental costume serves him very well, and the scene is set in a Palladian-style palace. One has only to compare this scene with Pellegrini's version of the same subject (fig. 85) to see how elaborate Tiepolo has become. Pellegrini is vague, though pathetic; but Tiepolo creates a grand structure—of people and architecture—about his Sophonisba. She is a public figure, acting out her drama before a large audience.

Operatic tendencies become yet more apparent in Tiepolo's later work. But the frescoes of Palazzo Dugnani show how early he had evolved an idiom for dealing with historical subjects and how he had already created his idea of a ceiling-heaven which, with variations, was going to be repeated again and again. He never failed to respond to the demand to dissolve, as it were, the expanse of a ceiling into a sphere of light where the figures recede from us, higher and higher, into infinity.

It is as well that he was not daunted, for the immediate years from 1730 onwards found him increasingly employed. As well as work in Milan, Venice, Bergamo and Vicenza—whence he writes that he is working breathlessly day and night—he was painting altarpieces for Germany. And he would have gone to Stockholm to fresco the Royal Palace, if the Swedes had been able to pay his high price.

These were the years when Tiepolo's fame began to be established beyond Northern Italy; by 1736, for instance, he was well enough known at Vienna for him to be strongly recommended to the Swedish agent on the way to Venice to look for a painter for the Royal Palace; and his altarpieces were reaching Germany by 1739. The immense number and variety of commissions could only be undertaken with assistance, and Domenico Tiepolo was of course still too young at this time to be of help. But Tiepolo did have pupils who worked for some years in the studio, and certainly some of the altarpieces for humble parts of the Veneto were executed with the pupils' help. Probably from quite early he also had the help of the architectural painter Girolamo Mengozzi-Colonna who was to design and paint for him so many frameworks for frescoes and pictures. And all this time Domenico Tiepolo was growing up. Like his father he was early active; at sixteen years old he is mentioned by Francesco Algarotti as 'already beginning to follow in his father's footsteps'.

Contemporaries do not otherwise make any reference to the actual people employed in Tiepolo's studio; by and large, the studio remains a mystery to us, almost as mysterious as the apparent inexhaustibility of the master mind who ran it. A commission meant to most painters countless drawings, preparatory oil sketches, and so on. Such sketches are often preferable to the completed work in which vivacity has been lost, and this remains true of Tiepolo. But Tiepolo sometimes cuts through the whole business of preliminary drawings and produces simply a *modello*, an oil sketch which is to be the 'model' for the large picture and on which the painter has worked out—and solved—his problems. Speed and spontaneity have made such work by Tiepolo the nearest to his frescoes, and the freshness of it made it appreciated at the time. It was an age, as Diderot remarked, for preferring sketches since these leave the eye something to imagine for itself, like, he says, children looking at cloud shapes. In Tiepolo's case a whole series of sketches related to a composition were often produced, but only one of these would be the *modello*; the rest were variations upon the original theme, done perhaps *after* the completed large picture. The subject was of no importance, and little attempt was made to note the sketch's relationship to the final composition; it existed in its own right.

The actual *modello* was more important, since it was submitted to the patron who might comment on it and suggest alterations. The more finished the *modello* the more it too existed in its own right. When Sebastiano Ricci was once submitting a carefully executed *modello* he pointed out that this was really the original; the altarpiece to be derived from it would be the copy. And a busy painter might well be tempted to submit a *modello* totally from his own hand but have the large picture painted with studio help.

Tiepolo probably despatched to Germany a *modello* of, for example, his *Trinity appearing to S. Clement*, an altarpiece painted in the decade of 1730 for the Archbishop-Elector of Cologne, Clemens August, the patron of Piazzetta and Pittoni. What is almost certainly the *modello* (fig. 86) shows very little variation from the final altarpiece (fig. 87) which was for a chapel at Nymphenburg; and X-rays reveal that the *modello* was subject to very few alterations in the course of execution, being drawn in originally much as it appears now except that the figure of the Pope was larger and his head was not raised. There seem to be no preliminary drawings, and it would be untypical of Tiepolo if there were. From the first Tiepolo had his conception of the aged Pope to whom appears the radiant group of the Trinity with angels. But at least one other sketch does exist of S. Clement, probably by Tiepolo, and showing his martyrdom; perhaps that scene was rejected in favour of the vision of the Trinity which gives Tiepolo good opportunity for splendid and miraculous effects.

86. GIAMBATTISTA TIEPOLO: *The Trinity appearing to S. Clement*(?). London, National Gallery

The S. Clement altarpiece is not typical of the type of work Tiepolo was producing for Venetian churches—unfortunately—and a year or two later he was occupied by a very different religious commission. Whereas his great ability lay in creating a grand manner for sacred and historical personages, he was often called upon to express religious doctrine in more pathetic and human terms. After the brilliance

87. GIAMBATTISTA TIEPOLO: *The Trinity appearing to S. Clement*(?).
Munich, Alte Pinakothek

and enchantment of the S. Clement composition, his Passion canvases for S. Alvise at Venice administer a severe shock. He had already harked back to Veronese, but here he was to recall—without in any way coming near—the tragic religious pictures of Titian and Tintoretto.

There are two flanking pictures, of the *Crowning with Thorns* and the *Flagellation,*

O

88. GIAMBATTISTA TIEPOLO: *The Road to Calvary*. Venice, S. Alvise

and a large central *Road to Calvary* (fig. 88) which show Tiepolo passing from the extreme of drama into melodrama. In place of the almost arrogant unscathed Christ in the *Trinity before S. Clement*, is this broken Christ on the way to Calvary, felled under the weight of a sickeningly heavy cross, mocked by the watching orientals and mourned by S. Veronica huddled in shadow at the right. The picture has a hysterical intensity which becomes displeasing, and the scene is too effective to be moving. The mixture of brutality and theatricality which Tiepolo has forced from himself as required by the subject aroused the not incomprehensible disgust of Ruskin. He thought the pictures might well be 'the product of a modern Parisian academy student', one who had read George Sand and Dumas. Even in the midst of rage, Ruskin kept a disconcerting shrewdness about pictures; the melodramatics of the *Road to Calvary* are very near nineteenth-century academic and oleographic treatment of religious scenes: that cloying rhetoric which is fluent and seems false. Ruskin means to hint that Tiepolo is insincere. That is untrue and too simple.

89. GIAMBATTISTA TIEPOLO: *The Madonna of Mount Carmel*. Venice, Scuola dei Carmini

Tiepolo was almost certainly sincere. But he was not the realist which he tried to be here, with many backward glances not only at sixteenth-century Venetian art but also at Rembrandt. The healthy, cheerful people, dignified, well-dressed, of his usual imagining are pageant-people; what he has produced at S. Alvise are wax-works from the chamber of horrors. The spectacle is degrading, and the trumpets and horses and Roman eagles make a distasteful carnival of the road to Calvary. The three pictures are Tiepolo's most elaborate Passion compositions, and their religious grand-guignol atmosphere makes clear his unsuitability to deal with violent and horrific themes, whatever their source.

Only a few years after, he was given a religious commission at Venice much more sympathetic to him. At the Scuola del Carmine he decorated for the Carmelite con-fraternity a ceiling, the centre of which was to be 'a Madonna descending from Heaven, holding in her hand a sacred scapular which she proffers to S. Simon Stock'. The terms of the commission were accepted by Tiepolo in January 1740, but it was two or three years before the central picture and its surrounding ones of *Virtues* were finished. The *Madonna of Mount Carmel* (fig. 89) is a vision which eclipses the splendours even of S. Clement's vision; indeed, it is probably Tiepolo's greatest masterpiece in religious painting. He understood well enough what was required by the subject which was to some extent, one might say, *his* subject: an assuaging vision of the supernatural to mortals.

The scene which he specifically illustrates here was a vital moment in the history of the Carmelite order. The Virgin is said to have appeared on this occasion to S. Simon at Cambridge, though that detail has clearly not bothered Tiepolo. The scapular, two pieces of cloth joined by strings, is the means of obtaining an impor-tant indulgence according to a Papal Bull which is perhaps a forgery but which Tiepolo accepts: those who have worn the scapular will be liberated from Purgatory through the Madonna's intercession on the first Saturday after their death 'or as soon as possible'.

The comforting doctrine of this statement is carefully expressed in the painting. Purgatory lies all about S. Simon, and the litter of tombstones, skulls, and cloudy horrors of yawning graves contrast with the tall white figure of the Madonna triumphantly wielding aloft the Child and swept through the sky by attendant angels. The vision is almost a hallucination, and the figures of it are heightened beyond normality. We feel, and share, the saint's privilege as he crouches low before the air-borne apparitions; like him we seem annihilated before this infraction of Nature's order.

The picture certainly is a part of belief, shared by Tiepolo no doubt as strongly as he shared belief in Christ's sufferings and Christ as Son of God. Indeed, so pleased were the confraternity by his work that he was made a member of it, and could thus partake of its posthumous advantages. The S. Alvise picture presents a

90. GIAMBATTISTA TIEPOLO: *Caprice Landscape with Figures.* Etching.
London, British Museum

quite unmiraculous moment: when God was suffering as man, unaided by his divinity. But Tiepolo's mind is instinctively on the side of divinity, excited by triumphs, apotheoses and glories; he magnifies the whole conception of the Carmelite vision to his own more splendid dimensions whereby Cambridge sinks into being a Palladian-style cornice but heaven becomes a great space swept by agitated, graceful, feminine forms. In this world of celestial servants it is not the Madonna who holds the sacred scapular; the office is delegated to an angel who carries it in one hand while supporting the Madonna's draperies with another.

That picture was unveiled with public applause. At the same time Tiepolo had yet another and private vein, developed probably from his own drawings and sketches with some reminiscences of the etchings of Rembrandt and Castiglione. We have some reason for supposing that he also collected engravings by earlier artists like Dürer. In the years about 1740 he began to produce his own etchings, blended in subject from his fancy and from half-remembered fragments of other men's work: soldiers and orientals, obelisks and urns enchantingly mingled into 'caprices' (fig. 90). Ten of these etchings were published at the time, and later a further group were published. Nevertheless, these still little-studied works are private fantasies of the artist's, revealing almost an obsession with certain motifs which possess for him personal meaning and magic: in some ways equivalent to the inspired doodles which Leonardo repeated again and again in his note-books. They show Tiepolo escaping from the tyranny of subject matter, just as Guardi was to escape from the tyranny of the recognizable view of Venice into his 'caprices'.

From these years too, sometime in the decade of 1740–50, date Tiepolo's grandest profane decorations at Venice: the Antony and Cleopatra frescoes in the ballroom of Palazzo Labia. There are unfortunately no references to when exactly these were painted, and little reference to them by later connoisseurs—though Reynolds bothered to sketch the *Banquet of Cleopatra* in 1752. By the mid-nineteenth century the splendid room was virtually a ruin, a fact lamented by one of the few Venetians of the period to pay any attention to the last of the city's great painters.

The story of Antony and Cleopatra reaches its culmination in Tiepolo's work at Palazzo Labia. But this famous love affair, not previously popular with painters, had already preoccupied him and had resulted in drawings, oil sketches and at least one large painting, the Melbourne *Banquet of Cleopatra* (fig. 91). The 'Banquet', derived in subject from Pliny not Plutarch, had occasionally provided an opportunity for seventeenth-century Dutch painters to depict a luxurious festival of still life, with peacock-pies and silver dishes laid out on Persian carpets. Tiepolo is not interested in that *genre* aspect, but in the high drama of the moment when Cleopatra puts one of her fabulous pearls into the wine and astounds Antony by her reckless magnificence.

This aspect of the story fascinated Tiepolo, as did also the conception of the lovers greeting or saying farewell at a port. At Palazzo Labia the two conceptions are crystallized into two of Tiepolo's greatest frescoes; and they are there the chief scenes of an elaborate decorative scheme which has not only been left unexplained but has usually been left unnoticed as well. While the two frescoes face each other on opposite walls of the high, cube-like room, the ceiling is alive with allegorical figures, Time and Beauty and the Winds, and Pegasus springing white into Olympus. Ravishing colours complete the enchantment, colours hardly susceptible of description for they are personal to Tiepolo. In the *Banquet* Cleopatra wears a dress whose colour resembles some *robe de chambre* of Madame Swann's as Proust describes it: 'vieux rose, cerise, rose Tiepolo . . .' The combination of history and decoration which was initiated excitedly enough at Palazzo Dugnani reaches heroic proportions here, as a whole world of figures look down on the two lovers, themselves moving in spacious architectural constructions.

Each of the end walls, pierced already by real doors and windows, becomes merely a façade, a pillared screen with a tall central archway leading into the fresco itself (figs. 92–93). This achievement is Girolamo Mengozzi-Colonna's, and is his

91. GIAMBATTISTA TIEPOLO: *The Banquet of Cleopatra.* Melbourne, National Gallery of Victoria

92. Wall with Tiepolo's *Banquet of Cleopatra*. Venice, Palazzo Labia

masterpiece; such painter-collaborators cannot expect to be singled out for praise, but his decorations at Palazzo Labia quickly earned him special mention by at least one contemporary historian. And Algarotti in a fascinating letter of 1756 discussed the alliance of Mengozzi and Tiepolo, with reference to another scheme on which they collaborated, the Pisani villa at Mira. There, he says, all is harmony and shows that a third person must have composed the quarrels which 'in other enterprises

93. Wall with Tiepolo's *Meeting of Antony and Cleopatra*. Venice, Palazzo Labia

those two famous painters have had'. No enterprise between them had until then been greater than Palazzo Labia; were their quarrels equally great?

Mengozzi-Colonna must also have been the designer and painter of the architectural setting of the Melbourne *Banquet*, a setting elaborate but enclosed. The same scene at Palazzo Labia (fig. 94) is a complicated triumph of suggested space: steps lead through the façade up to a semi-circular platform where the actual banquet is set. This area is encircled but not enclosed by a row of double columns which support the gallery where the musicians play; beyond, against the chalky blue sky, rise the pediment of a temple and a tapering silhouette of a single obelisk. The eye quickly penetrates the painted scaffolding of Mengozzi-Colonna, led into the scene by such trick effects as the dwarf on the simulated steps, and comes to rest at the base of the obelisk where in fact is Cleopatra's hand with the pearl.

To an earlier age even the subject might have seemed vulgar. But Tiepolo delights in its ostentation and its romantic qualities; there is nothing of high Roman terms in his treatment of it, and little that is specifically Egyptian either. Although the story derives from Pliny, this does not hinder Tiepolo from evolving out of the joint consul with Antony, Plancus, the bizarre oriental figure seated at the left of the table; and in the opposite fresco of *Antony and Cleopatra at the harbour* one of the flags gaily bears the German eagle. The impression rather than exact fact is what matters; ostentation is suggested, not painted literally. The location of Egypt is conveyed by the obelisk and a pair of statues; the attendant soldiers are indicated simply by the shafts of halberds rising into the sky; and down the long vista of the scene the two lovers confront each other.

Perhaps, as has recently been suggested, there are intended overtones of Venice itself in Cleopatra: just as the queen beguiled the man who had come to conquer her, so Venice in its splendour would beguile the Barbarians who plotted to destroy the Republic. What is perhaps more fundamental and certain is that Cleopatra, like Armida in the story of Rinaldo, is one of those enchantress-women whom the eighteenth century enjoyed and detested; at her worst (morally) this type of seductress is Madame de Merteuil in 'Les Liaisons Dangereuses'. Cleopatra lured on a great man to his fall, and the *Banquet* shows her beginning to weave her spell about him. There is a moral here, and a tragedy also, for as Dryden says 'the chief persons represented were famous patterns of unlawful love; and their end accordingly was unfortunate'. Perhaps the last person to paint the subject, Stothard, did so in strongly moral terms; it represented 'Intemperance' (but whose is not clear).

Whereas the *Banquet* had been the subject of a large picture before it became a fresco, the *Harbour Scene* (fig. 95) was virtually Tiepolo's first and final large-scale treatment of the subject. The treatment of it seems rather freer, and possibly it was painted rather later than the *Banquet*. However fast Tiepolo worked, Mengozzi-Colonna (perhaps with assistance) had, on each wall, a considerable task to finish first; and there may well have been some interval for Tiepolo between the two chief scenes. The *Harbour Scene* is conceivably meant to show Cleopatra's landing after her triumphal progress up the river Cydnus, but Tiepolo does not bother to give very precise indications. The lovers advance—Cleopatra in patterned white brocade; their splendid cortège is suggested in small space by massed heads and one single noble horse; and behind them a gang-plank leads to the shell-like prow of a ship.

94. GIAMBATTISTA TIEPOLO: *The Banquet of Cleopatra*. Venice, Palazzo Labia

95. GIAMBATTISTA TIEPOLO: *The Meeting of Antony and Cleopatra*. Venice, Palazzo Labia

96. GIAMBATTISTA TIEPOLO: *The Winds* (detail). Venice, Palazzo Labia

Suggestions of a whole fleet are conveyed by purely theatrical means: brief glimpses of a mast and tackle and the huge sheet of a billowing sail. The space of sky here seems really wet and windy. The façade frame of the fresco rises nearly to the ceiling, and there at its top astride the clouds the Winds themselves puff their cheeks to fill the sails (fig. 96). The *Banquet* is an immobile and tense scene; but the other wall is all movement, from the lovers who swing out towards the room to the flapping flags and prancing horses who emphasize the restless shifting pageant.

These frescoes are the high point of Tiepolo's decorative art in Venice. Magnificent fresco-schemes still lay before him in another twenty years of activity; but fresco-schemes outside Venice. In 1750, with Palazzo Labia presumably completed, he set out for his first journey abroad: to Würzburg, where the newly built Residenz of the Prince-Bishop was to be decorated by him with the help not only of Domenico but also of his younger son, Lorenzo, then fourteen. Tiepolo had not agreed to take this commission without hard bargaining, but the Prince-Bishop gained Tiepolo's greatest masterpieces: the fresco scenes connected with Frederick Barbarossa in the Kaisersaal of the Residenz; and, vaster in extent and even more superb in effect, the Grand Staircase ceiling fresco. Despite heavy bombing of the Residenz in the second world war, the central block still stands intact and it is this portion which contains Tiepolo's frescoes.

The Kaisersaal was the commission which had brought Tiepolo to Würzburg. Superb as the frescoes there are, they are enhanced by the magnificent rococo room, designed by Balthasar Neumann, with its multicoloured marble columns and its graceful windows looking over the Residenz garden (fig. 98). The ensemble in fact eclipses either architecture or frescoes individually, until one turns from the star-patterned marble floor to the ceiling where Frederick Barbarossa's bride is conveyed across the heavens by Apollo (fig. 99), dazzling interpretation by Tiepolo of Dark Age history. Nothing could be finer tribute to him than that he managed to produce great works of art out of the teutonically-learned programme drawn up by the local court-historian, whose idea of a fascinating subject was the homage paid by the Prince-Bishop Harold von Hocheim to Frederick Barbarossa at Würzburg in the twelfth century. Ignorant but imaginative, Tiepolo placed the scene firmly in sixteenth-century Venice, where in fact for him all history took place.

It was by a new contract, signed at Würzburg on 29th July 1752, that he agreed to fresco the staircase ceiling and accept twelve thousand florins for the task. No photographs unfortunately can give a proper conception of the ceiling as a whole, nor of the effect on the visitor slowly climbing the staircase as the vast fresco gradually expands before him. The decorative marriage here of architecture, stucco work, and fresco, eclipses even the Kaisersaal. Other enchanting German rococo palaces exist; no other is frescoed by Tiepolo. Yet the fact that in them even mediocre frescoes take on some beauty and grace, is oblique tribute to the genius of men like Neumann who created architectural settings which flatter the mediocre and enhance the great. And so here, the staircase with its alternations of statues, vases, and lamps, guides one by easy stages to the landing where inevitably one pauses. Above, nothing less than the four Continents of the world are assembled to do homage to the reigning Prince-Bishop, Carl Philipp von Greiffenklau, whose ermine-draped portrait is upheld by *putti* while Fame trumpets his name to the ends of the earth (fig. 97).

The extraordinary apotheosis of this petty and unimpressive person, one of a long line of Prince-Bishops whom the world has forgotten, is a triumph of sentiment over reason. So absurd, indeed, is it to suppose that the Continents would ever pay any attention whatsoever to Carl Philipp von Greiffenklau that the conception is almost imaginative. And, after all, the four Continents find themselves solemnly disposed at the base of the Albert Memorial. It was clearly quite unembarrassing to Tiepolo, who has, munificently enough, given the Prince-Bishop the fame he desired. Within fifty years of the fresco being painted, events were going to make

97. GIAMBATTISTA TIEPOLO: *Portrait of the Prince-Bishop* (detail of Staircase Fresco).
Würzburg, Residenz

absolute princes rather less sure of themselves, and the simplicity of mind which ordered this ceiling fresco is almost medieval in its anachronism. Not for nothing, one might say, had the Prince-Bishop invoked the twelfth-century shade of Frederick Barbarossa in the Kaisersaal.

Yet the ceiling's iconography is not totally personal to the Prince-Bishop, for there was already a considerable tradition of representing in paintings and in tapestries the four Continents, groups offering every opportunity for the splendid and the exotic. Tiepolo's grandly grouped pageants of elephants and Orientals, laden with the produce of their countries, do not fail in the exotic. But the idiom is uniquely his own, and in the midst of Eastern trappings and Asian refinements there are, for example, the sixteenth-century-costumed page boys of his usual imagining (fig. 100). And the detail of the iridiscent striped sleeve here is one slight indication of Tiepolo's felicitous touch which kept the whole vast scheme fresh and lively and marvellously effortless. Slightly out of the true centre of the heavens, at the point from which radiates the light which touches the groups of Continents, Apollo himself (fig. 101) stands in mid-air. Everything finally comes to this radiant circle and to the god who is the light of that world, the still centre around whom revolve the *putti*, the Personifications, the Continents, even Carl Philipp von Greiffenklau. It is, in the end, the apotheosis of Apollo that we witness; and he as god of the sunlight may be claimed as Tiepolo's god. The Würzburg ceiling is an

98. *View of the Kaisersaal. Würzburg, Residenz*

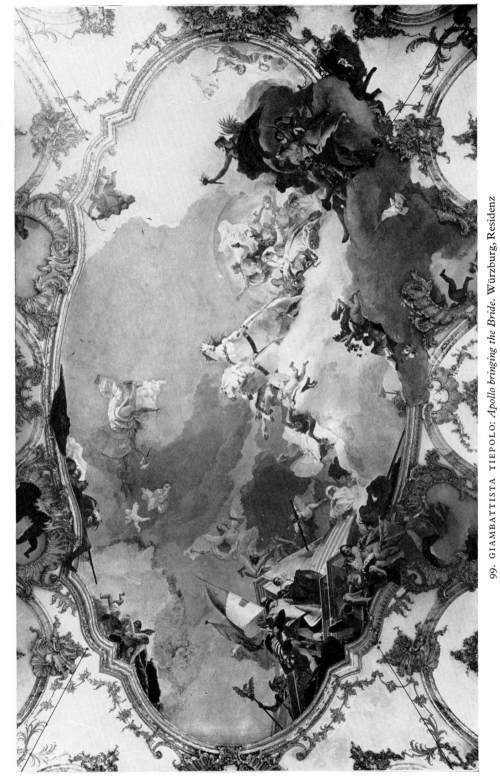

99. GIAMBATTISTA TIEPOLO: *Apollo bringing the Bride*. Würzburg, Residenz

P

100. GIAMBATTISTA TIEPOLO: *Page Boy* (detail of Staircase Fresco). Würzburg, Residenz

ode in his praise; not imperceptively has it been claimed as Tiepolo's Sistine chapel.

In 1753 the vast task was finished, and in the November of that year the painter and his two sons set off for Venice. At Würzburg Domenico Tiepolo had not only collaborated with his father, but had undertaken by himself the painting of over-doors in the Kaisersaal. Although he served loyally, and adequately pastiched both his father's matter and manner, he was not of course that type of painter at heart.

101. GIAMBATTISTA TIEPOLO: *Apollo* (detail of Staircase Fresco). Würzburg, Residenz

At Würzburg not only did he begin to have opportunities to show his real talent, but perhaps something of his more intimate style began to influence his father. Giambattista Tiepolo was now fifty-seven, and probably did not expect ever again to work on such an extended scale as at Würzburg. A tendency becomes apparent in him over the following years for more intimate treatment: of mythology and of religion. Perhaps that tendency was initiated by Domenico.

Two years after the return to Venice Tiepolo was elected President of the Venetian Academy. Piazzetta had died in 1754 while the Academy was still more of an idea than an established fact. And now Tiepolo was created its first President, for Piazzetta's title had been Director. The year of Tiepolo's election is perhaps the *annus mirabilis* of his career and his fame. It was also the year of Winckelmann's appearance on the literary scene: with a work on how to imitate the ancients in art. Taste was shifting, and Winckelmann's slim learned volume is an early sign of that shift. At Venice Tiepolo was busily employed as ever: so busy that he seems never to have bothered to obey the Academy's rule of presenting a reception piece. Indeed, though its first President, and the first painter of Venice, he seems to have had no relations with it once the three-year term of his presidency was ended.

As for the tendency towards an intimate and even tender treatment of heroic themes, this finds expression in some of the scenes in the fresco series for Villa Valmarana, outside Vicenza, painted about 1757. Domenico's contribution to the series—the rooms of the guest house—has already been discussed. In the villa itself Giambattista Tiepolo frescoed the hall and the four downstairs rooms that lead off it. The Iliad and the Æneid, the *Gerusalemma Liberata* and the *Orlando Furioso* provided the subjects for the four rooms. Bettinelli, a poet of the day and one who had praised Tiepolo, explains in his *Dell'Entusiasmo delle Belle Arti* (1769) that what makes these poems immortal are 'le passioni d'Achille, di Didone, d'Orlando, di Tancrede. . . .' These are virtually the moving emotional subjects Tiepolo chose. In this way he becomes almost a historian of the sort Bettinelli mentions, whose duty is to paint 'come in gran quadri' great personages in such a way that we seem to be present 'at a theatrical performance excellently played by excellent actors'. In the hall a whole long wall is decorated with one last great treatment of the 'sacrifice' theme, *The Sacrifice of Iphigenia* (fig. 102). Here Tiepolo sounds the drums and trumpets of his grandest manner in the most perfect treatment of a theme which had often occupied him. It is a bloodless operatic drama, for even as Iphigenia raises her eyes to heaven in a last plea Diana herself appears on the ceiling. The effect of theatre is heightened by this relationship of wall to ceiling whereby the whole room becomes, as it were, a stage. The front door of the villa opens on to this scene, the visitor steps at once out of the everyday world of a garden on a hillside near Vicenza into this illusionistic and static moment where for ever Iphigenia's sacrifice is arrested at the altar by divine intervention.

But in the small villa rooms Tiepolo adopts a simpler and more poignant manner. Taking a subject hardly ever, if indeed ever at all treated by another painter, he achieves in *Achilles on the Seashore* (fig. 103) a sort of inlet into the poetry and pathos of Homer's world. The hero mourns by the seashore—though the seashore is no more than an artificial platform—and his mother rises from the grey sea to comfort him. There are here no flourishes of the rococo, no drama; no triumph even. Under

102. GIAMBATTISTA TIEPOLO: *The Sacrifice of Iphigenia*. Vicenza, Villa Valmarana

103. GIAMBATTISTA TIEPOLO: *Achilles on the Seashore*. Vicenza, Villa Valmarana

the shadow of towering rocks Thetis and her Nereid companion gaze mournfully at
the brooding hero; and the note of pagan sadness looks back to early Renaissance
treatment of classical story: to Botticelli not to Veronese.

104. GIAMBATTISTA TIEPOLO: *Mars and Venus*. Vicenza, Villa Valmarana

Other frescoes at Valmarana are gayer or more dramatic. But the poignancy of the *Achilles* prepares the way for the poignant human feeling behind so many of Tiepolo's late religious pictures. In the single room he frescoed in the Valmarana guest house, he chose *Olympus* as the subject: so many softly tinted clouds cover the walls, amid which recline the charming insouciant figures of his gods and goddesses, themselves so free from any serious classical overtones. In the midst of Domenico's scenes of everyday life, Giambattista assembled a pantheon and an anthology of the persons who had haunted him for so long, men heroic and healthy in armour and women with blonde flesh and hair, buoyant and at ease like the group of *Mars and*

Venus (fig. 104). Four years later Anton Raphael Mengs was going to execute his cold seriously classical *Parnassus* (fig. 105) for Villa Albani at Rome: frigid rebuke to the excesses of the rococo which was already marked as doomed. And a few years later still, Mengs and Tiepolo were to meet in rivalry at Madrid.

For Tiepolo remained as active as ever. After the Vicenza stay, he was at Udine, then at Verona, then busy on a large ceiling for the country villa of the Pisani family at Strà. In March 1761 he spoke of this task as the most important of all his commissions; at the same time he was working on a large canvas for the Russian court and two pictures for S. Marco at Rome, as well as (probably) a portrait of Algarotti. But already a still larger task was being prepared. Charles III of Spain needed a painter for the vast rooms of the newly built royal palace at Madrid. He appealed for Tiepolo, and appealed through his ambassador at Venice for the Senate to expedite Tiepolo's journey to Spain. Tiepolo delayed, busy—and perhaps reluctant—as he was. But by December 1761 he was resigned to going, and in the spring of the following year he set out on the longest and the last journey of his life.

Ill and tired, he reached Madrid in June. There he once again repeated, on the huge throne room ceiling, his vision of the heavens: this time an apotheosis of the last great absolute monarchy, that of Spain. Once more provinces drag their offerings of tribute, Apollo bestrides the cloud, Spain (in the person of Neptune) rules the waves. Two more ceilings were painted in the royal palace, with the help of Domenico and Lorenzo Tiepolo.

Tiepolo had completed the mission for which he had come. Yet he showed no haste to return home. Very early in 1767 the question was put to him directly: would he rather return or stay in Spain? He chose to stay, thanking the King for his clemency; and on Tiepolo's letter of reply the King noted: *esta bien.* Although Charles went on to make a memorandum to give Tiepolo work, it was the painter who had, after some time, to draw respectful attention to his own idleness. The Spanish tactics of silence and delay were already weaving an atmosphere of unease about the ageing painter. The King's confessor favoured the rival artist Mengs, whom Charles had previously patronized; and when finally Tiepolo received the commission for seven altarpieces at Aranjuez it was a shortlived triumph. The altarpieces were hardly in position before they were removed and the commission assigned this time to Mengs and two Spanish painters.

The damaged and mutilated altarpieces by Tiepolo survive, dispersed in various parts of the world. Undamaged there also survive the *modelli* for some of the altarpieces, and these show the nervous, almost tragic handling of Tiepolo's late style. He still at times thinks in terms of glories and visions: an angel appears with the Host to S. Pascal Baylon, angels float through the pillared room where S. Charles Borromeo is in ecstasy before the Crucifix. Yet the subjects are no longer excuses

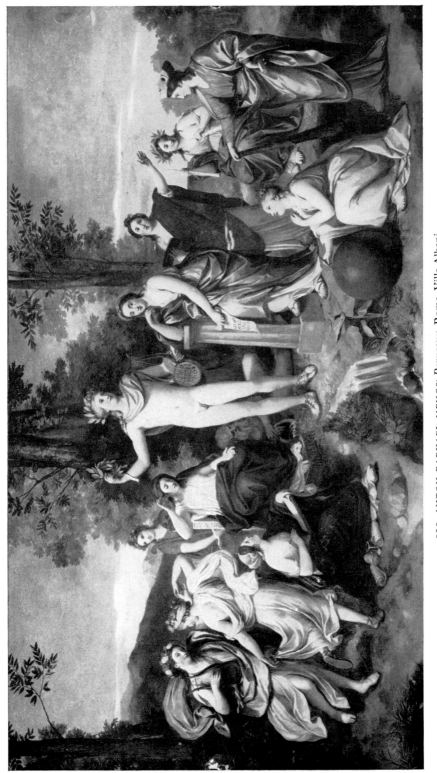

105. ANTON RAPHAEL MENGS: *Parnassus*. Rome, Villa Albani

for grand displays of celestial pageants, but treated with a quite new intensity of feeling; an agitation which is felt in the flickering touches of paint and in the faces of the saints, fretted by the agony of devotion.

A scene like the *Stigmata of S. Francis* (fig. 106)—a subject Tiepolo had probably painted once many years before for a Venetian church—is pathetic not grandiloquent. The angel is borne on no splendid sweep of cloud, nor surrounded by a circle of cherubs; instead, he embraces with a consoling gesture the saint seated in a harsh and arid landscape, and the stigmata's infliction is treated almost as a human ordeal. Tiepolo had tried a way of treating religious subjects in human terms in the S. Alvise Passion picture, but without simplicity or poignancy. Human suffering was there a spectacle. His late small sketches are moving because so unmelodramatic. The *S. Francis* could hardly well be quieter or less rhetorical in its suggestions of the loneliness of sanctity; and the frail wooden cross, drawn with nervously fluid strokes of the brush, rises tall into the empty sky like a symbol of that loneliness.

In another very late sketch painted in Spain, the *Deposition* (fig. 107), the subject has resulted in a more stark and intensely tragic scene. Domenico had painted a number of versions of the subject in which the story is illustrated literally: orientals and soldiers, the thieves on their crosses, and a reconstructed Jerusalem behind. But Giambattista's is not an illustration; it is a meditation on the story, mystic not literal. So there are no human mourners or spectators except S. John and the Virgin; even the thieves' crosses are bare. Instead, the corpse of Christ is mourned and tended by angels, while the Virgin raises her grief-stricken face to heaven, seated as it were in eternal sorrow. Christ's suffering and death become timeless, as in those early Renaissance pictures where the Passion is set outside Florence or some other recognizable city; here the setting is Spain and in the background, between the crosses, appear the buildings of Madrid.

On 27th March 1770 Tiepolo died suddenly. His two sons parted immediately after: Lorenzo remaining in Spain until his death, Domenico setting off home for Venice. And Tiepolo's world died with him. No one was to attempt its resurrection, though the style continued to be reflected at Venice in the pale imitations of minor men. He died in a foreign country which was perhaps the only country left in Europe where he could be welcome, and even there he had met with opposition and neglect.

The greatest imaginative painter of the age was really outside the standards his age erected to judge painters. When Cochin said of one of Tiepolo's ceilings that it was 'more beautiful than natural' he indicated, as he thought, its failing. And against this canon of 'Nature', the great artists of the eighteenth century were often to seem culpable and even ridiculous. In England Gainsborough's portraits were to be called 'daubs'; in France Voltaire sneered at Watteau's work and Diderot said he

106. GIAMBATTISTA TIEPOLO: *The Stigmata of S. Francis*.
London, Count Antoine Seilern collection

107. GIAMBATTISTA TIEPOLO: *The Deposition*. Zürich, Private collection

would give *ten* Watteau's for a single Teniers. Tiepolo was, then, exercising his imagination in a chilly climate of critical appraisal. He might be popular with his compatriots, with aristocratic patrons in *retardière* countries; but two of his chief pictorial sources—religion and mythology—were themselves going out of favour. An age of scrutiny, as the eighteenth century supremely was, could hardly be expected to take Tiepolo's work seriously, and the more imaginative he was the more he invited criticism.

Canaletto and Guardi, the two Longhi, and Rosalba, all have some value as evokers of their city and century. Tiepolo, so much greater than any of them, stands outside Venice and the eighteenth century. His personality too is apart, emerges little from documents of the time, and was left unrecorded even factually since he was never the subject of sustained biography until long after his death. Like every genius he is a mystery and would remain one even if we possessed, for instance, as many of his letters as we do of Mozart's.

But though he stands so far above and beyond eighteenth-century Venice, he is really the best excuse for paying it serious attention. His art alone of all the art practised in the city at the time can claim uniqueness. And whatever the misconceptions about the frivolity of Venice, its triviality, its superficiality, Tiepolo corrects them all: not by lengthy argument but by the sustained example of his work.

NOTES

BRIEF BIBLIOGRAPHY

ACKNOWLEDGEMENTS

INDEX

NOTES

For bibliography on the painters discussed in the text, the reader is referred firstly to that given under each in Thieme-Becker, *Lexikon*, supplemented by the very full and up-to-date bibliographies in C. Donzelli, *Pittori Veneziani del Settecento*, 1957 (where illustrations of pictures by the majority of painters discussed here will also be found). The notes below do not attempt to duplicate Donzelli's work; nor do they aim specifically at filling gaps in his bibliographies.

Introduction

For eighteenth-century Venice in general, see, among other works (many not available in England): S. Romanin, *Storia Documentata di Venezia*, VIII, 1859; W. Carew Hazlitt, *The Venetian Republic*, 1900 ed., II; M. Berengo, *La Società Veneta alla fine del Settecento*, 1956 (particularly important).

Algarotti's comment on Italy's place in the world is in his *Pensieri Diversi, Opere*, 1764 ed., VII, p. 42. On the Inquisition, see G. Comisso, *Les Agents Secrets de Venise au XVIIIᵉ siècle*, 1944 ed. Northcote's shock is recorded in *Memorials of an Eighteenth-Century Painter* (ed. S. Gwynn), 1898, p. 179. Abbé Richard's comment in *Description . . . de l'Italie*, 1766, II, p. 419, note (*a*). For da Ponte's account of his escapade, see his *Memoirs* (ed. L. A. Sheppard), 1929, pp. 67/8. Da Ponte claims in fact that everyone else feared for him, but that he was sure he would be safe. The uproar occasioned by his verses is worth study by anyone supposing the climate of the city to have been liberal. Casanova records his own attempted paradox with Voltaire in his *Mémoires* (and also some sub-acid comments on Algarotti): the passage conveniently in E. Bonora, *Letterati, Memorialisti e Viaggiatori del Settecento*, 1951, p. 739. Berengo, *op. cit.*, p. 195, has well observed how even the adventurers of the period at Venice, like da Ponte and Casanova, did not become political rebels.

On the chaos of the archives, see Romanin, *op. cit.*, p. 114: in 1761 three *Corettori alle Leggi* were appointed to deal with such questions and to propose a variety of reforms (but they had difficulty in agreeing with each other). On the book trade, see H. Brown, *The Venetian Printing Press*, 1891, pp. 193 ff., 'it (book trade) was choked by a multiplicity of laws relating to every conceivable phase of its existence' (p. 195); also G.

Morazzoni, *Il Libro Illustrato Veneziano del Settecento*, 1943; by 1765 Gasparo Gozzi thought a crisis had been reached (Morazzoni, *op. cit.*, p. 51). Maffei's *Consiglio Politico* was first published in 1797; the title page says, 'presentato al governo veneto nell'anno 1736.' Further discussion in G. Silvestri, *Un Europeo del Settecento: Scipione Maffei*, 1954, pp. 169 ff. The instructions given to the French ambassador in 1786 are quoted by Berengo, *op. cit.*, p. 10, note 2.

Connoisseurs and Patrons

L'idea generale delle scienze is singled out by G. Natali, *Storia Letteraria d'Italia: Il Settecento*, 1929, I, p. 241. For Mariette's interest in contemporary Venetian painting, see especially his letters to Temanza published in the original (for the first time) by E. Müntz, *Les Archives des Arts*, 1890, pp. 101 ff.

For the Président de Brosses' list, see his *Lettres Familières sur l'Italie* (ed. Y. Brizard), 1931, I, pp. 205 ff. Nor will Tiepolo's name be found for instance in any eighteenth-century editions of M. Pilkington's *Dictionary of Painters* (first ed. 1770); nor in Fuseli's revised edition of 1805 *sqq*. The complaints of Bergeret and Fragonard are in their *Journal inédit* (ed. Tornézy), 1895, p. 394; Cochin's comment in the *Voyage d'Italie*, 1758, III, p. 46.

Vincenzo da Canal's *Vita di Lazzarini* was published by G. A. Moschini in 1809. His treatise *Maniera del depingere moderno* was published in 1810: for it and da Canal further, see N. Ivanoff in *Arte Veneta*, 1953, pp. 117 ff. Gradenigo's notes on artistic events published by L. Livan, *Notizie d'Arte*, 1942. Gasparo Gozzi's *Gazzetta Veneta* (1760) became in 1761 the *Osservatore Veneta;* for this aspect of his career, see for example G. de Beauvillé, *Gasparo Gozzi Journaliste Vénitien*, 1937. Baretti's comment is cited by G. Ortolani, *Voci e Visioni del Settecento Veneziano*, 1926, p. 26, who attempts to minimize it. Gozzi on the book trade, cited by Morazzoni, *loc. cit., supra*.

Strange's letter of 1789 to Sasso is quoted by F. Mauroner in *Arte Veneta*, 1947, I, p. 49. Mariette's in Müntz, *op. cit.*, p. 133. For Ricci's drawings after Watteau: A. Blunt and E. Croft-Murray, *Venetian Drawings at Windsor Castle*, 1957, pp. 61 ff. Some information about Pellegrini acting for Rosalba, and the mention of Zanetti staying at Mr. Smith's, is in the important group of letters to and from Rosalba, published by V. Malamani in *Le Gallerie Nazionali Italiane*, IV, 1899, pp. 27 ff. See for these points *op. cit.*, pp. 112 and 117.

For the elder Zanetti see G. Lorenzetti in *Miscellanea di Storia Veneta*, 1917 (extract); further (with comment on his caricatures) see E. Croft-Murray, *op. cit., supra*, pp. 146 ff. For a portrait of him by Rosalba, see T. Pignatti in *Bollettino dei Musei Civici Veneziani*, 1956, pp. 53 ff. On the younger Zanetti's aesthetics, see M. Pittaluga in *L'Arte*, 1918, pp. 5 ff. and N. Ivanoff in *Atti dell' Istituto Veneto*, 1952/3. In general for the two Z. see also F. Borroni in *Amor di Libro*, 1955 (IV), pp. 195 ff., and *ib.* 1956 (I), pp. 12 ff.

For Joseph Smith, see K. T. Parker's introduction to his *Canaletto Drawings at Windsor Castle*, 1948, and A. Blunt's introduction, *op. cit.* The Longhi of Murray and his family was included in Joseph Smith's sale, London, 17 May (2nd day), 1776 (lot 81).

On Algarotti: I. F. Treat, *F.A. Un Cosmopolite au 18ᵉ siècle*, 1913; also M. Siccardi, *A. Critico e Scrittore di Belle Arti*, 1910 (neither very satisfactory, though considerable *MS.* references in Treat); G. Fogolari in *Bollettino d'Arte*, 1911, for some eighteenth-century Venetian pictures belonging to A. For A. and Dresden see L. Ferrari, *L'Arte*, 1900, pp. 150 ff.; and especially H. Posse in Prussian *Jahrbuch*, 1931 (Appendix); for the *Flora* (now at San Francisco) see M. Levey, *The Burlington Magazine* (XCIX), 1957, pp. 89 ff. Satiric comment on A. by his contemporary Girolamo Zanetti (and also complaint that A. is despoiling Venice) is in Z.'s *Memorie* published by F. Stefani in *Archivio Veneto*, 1885, pp. 93 ff. A.'s comment on Maser: Bottari-Ticozzi, *Lettere Artistiche*, 1822, VII, pp. 461 ff. For A.'s own engravings: A. Ravà, *L'Arte*, 1913, pp. 58 ff. Apart from Liotard's pastel of A. (reproduced in Posse, *loc. cit.*), his appearance is recorded in two drawings by Jonathan Richardson (senior) of 1736: see *Portrait Drawings* (Victoria & Albert Museum booklet), 1953, pl. 13, and also R.A. exhibition, *Paul Oppé Collection*, 1958 (No. 119).

On the satires directed at profane-style religious pictures see the unsatisfactorily brief reference of V. Malamani, *Il Settecento a Venezia, I: la Satira del Costume*, 1891 ed., p. 110.

The Painters

For the Venetian Academy: E. Bassi, *La R. Accademia di Belle Arti di Venezia*, 1941; and for its having lost Zuccarelli, Bassi, *op. cit.*, pp. 71/2. A good deal of useful information about the Academy was published by G. Fogolari in *L'Arte*, 1913, pp. 241 ff. Exhibitions in eighteenth-century Venice to be discussed in a forthcoming article by F. Haskell & M. Levey, *Arte Veneta*, 1958. Cochin's summing up, *op. cit.*, p. 159.

I: The History Painters

For Lessing on the musical pictures in Dryden's *Ode* 'die den Pinsel müssig lassen', see *Laokoon*, 1881 ed., p. 95.

For Algarotti's choice of Dryden's *Ode* as subject for Tiepolo, see Posse, *op. cit.*, p. 50, note 1. Some frescoes by Longhi are in S. Pantaleon at Venice; more disastrous still perhaps is his ceiling for Palazzo Grassi, also in Venice. Canaletto's *Holy Family* is recorded by L. Crico, *Lettere sulle Belle Arti Trevigiane*, 1833, p. 297. In a

London sale of 1766 (*i.e.* during his lifetime) Anon, 5 February (lot 41), was Canaletto, *A small picture of a flower and a bird;* lot 42, ditto, *its companion.*

Freud's comments are in *Totem and Taboo* (transl. A. A. Brill), 1942 ed., p. 95; Valéry's *Pièces sur l'Art*, 1934, p. 104, for his summing up of these Veneto villas. Louis XIV's letter quoted in full by F. J. B. Watson, *Wallace Collection Catalogues: Furniture*, 1956, p. xxvi.

For some Veronese-style decorations on porcelain (Vezzi factory) see Arthur Lane, *Italian Porcelain*, 1954, pl. 11 C; his pl. 21 C shows a piece of Cozzi porcelain with Veronese's *Rape of Europa* (and Tintoretto and Tiepolo (?) medallions round it).

De la Fosse's snub to Ricci is reported by Walpole, *Anecdotes . . .* , III, 1826, p. 282. Marco Ricci's letter to Gaburri is in Bottari-Ticozzi, *Lettere Artistiche*, 1822, II, pp. 129/30; S. Ricci's confession of his lust for cheese, Bottari-Ticozzi, *op. cit.*, IV, p. 96. The letter about 'Rizzi of Venice' is quoted by F. J. B. Watson, *Arte Veneta*, 1954, p. 295, note 1. N. Passeri's *Del Metodo di Studiare la Pittura . . .* , 1795, I, pp. 158 ff., for Ricci's defects and danger.

On Pellegrini's and M. Ricci's scenery for *Pyrrhus* see M. Whinney & O. Millar, *English Art 1625–1714*, 1957, p. 307. For the chairs once at Kimbolton see the Duke of Manchester sale, Kimbolton, 18 July *sqq.*, 1949, pl. 3. Some appreciative comment on Pellegrini is in E. K. Waterhouse, *Painting in Britain 1530–1790*, 1953, p. 91; also Whinney & Millar, *op. cit.*, pp. 307 ff. The Johann Wilhelm allegories discussed and illustrated by M. Goering in the Munich *Jahrbuch*, 1937, pp. 233 ff. For the Banque de France ceiling described see *Vies des Premiers Peintres du Roi . . .* (ed. Lépicié), 1752, II., pp. 122 ff.

Amigoni's work at Moor Park (and other places in England) is early mentioned, in B. Gamba, *Galleria dei Letterati ed Artisti Illustri delle Provincie Veneziane*, 1822, *ad vocem*. For Lorenzi's supposed aid to the illiterate Tiepolo, see Molmenti, *G. B. Tiepolo*, 1909 ed., p. 35 (citing Zannandreis, *Vite dei Pittori . . . Veronesi*, 1891, p. 429). Walpole's unkind comments in his *Anecdotes . . .* , IV, 1827, p. 112 ff. For Amigoni supposedly producing decorative designs for furniture, see G. Morazzoni, *Mobili Veneziani Laccati*, 1954, I, p. 33.

For illustrated books of the period: G. Morazzoni, *Il Libro Illustrato Veneziano del Settecento*, 1943; and, much less useful, M. Lanckorońska, *Die Venezianische Buchgraphik des XVIII Jahrhunderts*, 1950.

Tessin's comments on various contemporary Venetian painters published by O. Sirén, *Dessins et Tableaux de la Renaissance Italienne dans les Collections de Suède*, 1902, pp. 103 ff. G. B. Albrizzi's *Memorie intorno alla vita di G. B. Piazzetta*, prefaced to his *Studi di pittura designati da G.B.P.*, 1760. Cochin, *op. cit.*, p. 137, for Piazzetta's *Death of Darius* in Palazzo Pisani.

Balestra's protests against the 'rococo': see his letters in Bottari-Ticozzi, *op. cit.*, II, *passim*.

For a provincial person's efforts to copy Tiepolo, see A. Ricci, *. . . Artisti di Ancona*, 1834, II, p. 369, on his relative Alessandro Ricci copying without realizing that Tiepolo 'è uno originale che difficilmente s'imita . . .'.

Algarotti's letter of 13 February 1751 (from Potsdam) to Mariette: Bottari-Ticozzi, *op. cit.*, VII, pp. 387 ff. Madame Geoffrin's comments on the picture commissioned from Vien, in *Correspondance inédite du Roi Stanislas-Auguste Poniatowski et Madame Geoffrin* (ed. C. de Mouÿ), 1875, pp. 218/9.

For G. A. Guardi's copy after Balestra (but not identified as such) see N. Coe in *Bulletin of Cleveland Museum*, November 1957, pp. 198 ff. The outline of events concerning the Angelo Raffaele organ given by T. Pignatti in *Arte Veneta*, 1950, pp. 144 ff. F. Guardi's Roncegno altarpiece discovered and published by M. Muraro in *The Burlington Magazine* [C], 1958, pp. 3 ff.

Guarana has been rather neglected by modern criticism. The Ospedaletto frescoes have never been properly published. A. Mengozzi Colonna signs and dates his share there (above the right-hand doorway): *Augustus Colonna Pin. Anno MDCCLXXVI.*

II: Landscape Painting

For the English attitude in general see E. Manwaring, *Italian Landscape in Eighteenth-Century England*, 1925.

On the Bolognese caprice landscape frescoes, see G. Zucchini, *Paesaggi e Rovine nella Pittura Bolognese del Settecento*, 1947; Girolamo Zanetti's comment in his *Memorie . . .* , *op. cit.*, p. 104.

For the 'Tombs', see T. Borenius, *Burlington Magazine* (LXIX), 1936, p. 245; E. Arslan, *Commentari*, July/September 1955, pp. 189 ff.; F. J. B. Watson, *Burlington Magazine* (XCV), 1953, pp. 362 ff. Four previously untraced Tombs from Goodwood were in Sir Humphrey de Trafford sale, London, 26 June 1957 (lots 53–55; Birmingham picture lot 54); another was in Ronald Avery sale, London, 14 May 1958 (lot 46). Walpole knew some of them: 'the stories being ill told . . . it is extremely difficult to decypher to what individual so many tombs, edifices and allegories belong in each respective piece,' *Anecdotes* . . . , IV, 1827, p. 116. Pignotti's *La Tomba di Shakespeare*, 1779, mentioned by G. Natali, *Storia Letteraria d'Italia: Il Settecento*, 1929, I, p. 594. Juvarra's 'Tombs' for the Ricci in Blunt & Croft Murray, *op. cit.*, pp. 41 ff.

Interesting comments on M. Ricci's gouache scenes, and indications of commissions to him, are given in a letter of 1761 from the elder Zanetti to Algarotti: 'li paesi a tempera di Marchetto Ricci che son difficiliss.mi a trovarsi . . . . ; Lorenzetti in *Misc' di Storia Veneta*, 1917, p. 138.

Gasparo Gozzi's letter to Caterina Dolfin Tron on town and country life ('. . . invece d'udire canti d'uccelletti, ho da sentire otto giorni continui le campane di S. Zaccaria che fanno allegrezza per una reverendissima Badessa . . .') in *Raccolta di Prose e Lettere scritte nel secolo XVIII*, 1830, II, p. 113.

On Zuccarelli and Wilson at Venice (and on Wilson's portrait of Z.) see forthcoming article by M. Levey in *Burlington Magazine*. Smith apparently possessed some classical landscapes by Z. (like the *Apollo and Daphne*, engraved by Wagner) which did *not* pass into the Royal Collection; perhaps they are the pictures by Z.

in the Smith sale of 1776. Z.'s sale of his work was in London, 10 February 1762; for it and Z.'s English career further, see M. Levey's forthcoming article in *Italian Studies*.

Algarotti's patronage recorded in Posse, *op. cit.* Baretti thinks of 'mio Z.' apropos the landscape outside Lisbon: *Lettere Familiari*, 1763, II, p. 8. Some mention of Z. bringing Algarotti's bequest to Chatham in F. Viglione, *L'Algarotti e l'Inghilterra*, 1919, p. 12. H. Angelo, *Reminiscences* . . . , 1904, *passim* for anecdotes and praise of Z. On this concept of Arcady, and Steele on pastoral poetry, see for example, M. M. Fitzgerald, *First Follow Nature*, 1947, p. 40. Carey's thought quoted by the Redgraves, *A Century of Painters* . . . , 1866, pp. 180 ff., with their own pejorative comments.

For pictures, probably by Antonio Diziani, owned by the Adam brothers, see their sale, London, 25 February 1773 (lots 1–2), where the pictures are attributed to 'Gas. Dizziano'. All the same, the subjects (*i.e. A Vintage* and *its companion*) suggest Antonio's work much more. Probably the two collaborated on large scale pictures, just as the Ricci had done.

Rosalba's scorn for Z. and Wilson recorded by an anecdote in *The Farington Diary* (ed. Greig), I, p. 55. Goethe's amazement quoted by L. Hautecoeur, *Rome et la Renaissance de l'Antiquité*, 1912, p. 179.

III: The View Painters

On the phenomenon of the Grand Tour, see for example W. E. Mead, *The Grand Tour in the Eighteenth Century*, 1914. For some idea of it in artistic terms, see the exhibition catalogue *Eighteenth-Century Italy and the Grand Tour*, Norwich, May/July 1958.

Fuseli's remarks on 'that last branch of uninteresting subjects, that kind of landscape which is entirely occupied by tame delineation of a given spot', cited and discussed by K. Clark, *Landscape into Art*, 1949 ed., p. 35. Goldoni on Venice: *Tutte le Opere: Mémoires* (ed. G. Ortolani), 1935, p. 35. Goethe's comment on the Doge in the *bucintoro: Italienische Reise* (*Goethes Werke*, XI), 1950 ed., p. 80.

For Canaletto's use of the *camera ottica* see T. Pignatti, *Il Quaderno di Disegni del Canaletto alle*

Gallerie di Venezia, 1958, where the whole question is authoritatively discussed. Early depictions of the Campanile: G. Fogolari in *Rassegna d'Arte*, 1912, pp. 49 ff.

Boschini calls Heintz ''l piu capricioso' in *La Carta del Navegar* . . . , 1660, p. 536. Balestra on Richter's *genio* in Bottari-Ticozzi, *op. cit.*, II, p. 123.

Marshal Schulenburg sale, London, 12 April 1775; the Foot's Cray reference published by F. J. B. Watson, *Burlington Magazine* (XCV), 1953, p. 206. Strange's sale (anonymous), London, 10 December 1789. Carlevaris' etchings, *Le Fabbriche e Vedute di Venezia* . . . , 1703; the dedication says the object is 'di rendere più facile alla notizia de Paesi stranieri le Venete Magnificenze . . .'.

For one aspect of the decline of Venice and rise of Savoy, see for instance E. P. Noether, *Seeds of Italian Nationalism 1700–1815*, 1951, p. 43; Noether, *op. cit.*, p. 24, for Campanella's striking phrase about Venice as a new Noah's ark. For Mr. Cole and the Earl of Manchester's embassy see W. Nisser, *Burlington Magazine* (LXX,) 1937, pp. 30 ff. Rawdon Brown's transcript and notes in the Public Record Office, London; see also M. Symonds, *Days spent on a Doge's Farm*, 1893, p. 21, for Pisani family picture of Venetian ambassador at the Tower of London. The Victoria & Albert sketchbook published by J. Pope-Hennessy in *Burlington Magazine* (LXXIII), 1938, pp. 126 ff. G. A. Moschini, *Della Letteratura Veneziana del Secolo XVIII . . .* , 1806, III, p. 87, for Carlevaris' supposed apoplectic death.

'*Scomunicò . . . il teatro*' is Zanetti's reporting of Canaletto's decision (*Della Pittura Veneziana*, 1771, p. 463). That C. has more 'work than he can doe' is reported by McSwiny in a letter of November 1727: see H. Finberg in *Walpole Society*, IX, 1921, p. 23. For the Conti pictures, see F. Haskell in *Burlington Magazine* (XCVIII), 1956, pp. 296 ff., correcting all previous statements. Views of the *Interior of S. Marco* (versions at Windsor and Montreal) are shown to be out of date by R. Gallo, *Atti dell' Istituto Veneto*, 1956–7 (offprint) who wrongly supposes the pictures to be early; they must be *ca.* 1750, if not later. Algarotti's commission to C. is discussed by him in a letter: Bottari-Ticozzi, *op. cit.*, VII, p. 429.

For Canaletto's Whitehall topography, see J. Hayes in *Burlington Magazine* (C), 1958, pp. 341 ff. Turner's attitude to C. cited by A. J. Finberg, *In Venice with Turner*, 1930, p. 80; Turner's picture, *op. cit.*, pl. XIV. For attitude to landscape painters at Rome: L. Hautecoeur, *op. cit.*, p. 154. The Crewe incident quoted by Watson, *Canaletto*, 1954, p. 9. Mrs. Thrale's comments in *Thraliana* (ed. K. C. Balderston), 1942, I, p. 536; as well as Canalettos she bought some pictures by Amigoni. For Angelica Kauffmann's will (relevant portion): Lady V. Manners and G. C. Williamson, *Angelica Kauffmann*,

1924, p. 244. Canova also collected some pictures by C.: G. A. Moschini, *op. cit.*, p. 77, note 1. Rose's comment in his *Letters from the North of Italy*, 1819, I, p. 272.

For Moretti: G. Delogu, *Pittori Veneti Minori . . .* , 1930; views by M. are mentioned as despatched to England by G. M. Sasso at Venice in a letter of 1789 to Sir A. Hume (MSS. in National Gallery archives).

Bellotto and Canaletto as *rinomatissimi* in 1743 according to Girolamo Zanetti's *Memorie* (ed. Stefani), *Archivio Veneto*, 1885, p. 145. For B.'s post-Italian activity see especially the exhibition catalogue *Bernardo Bellotto . . .* , Whitechapel, 1957.

For Costa's work discussed and illustrated fully: M. Pittaluga, *Acquafortisti Veneziani del Settecento*, 1953, pp. 75 ff. Ruskin's disapproval of the Brenta villas is stated in *The Stones of Venice*, 1851, I, pp. 344/5.

The Windsor *View towards Murano* is discussed by Watson in *Arte Veneta*, 1955, p. 260 ff., and again in *Arte Veneta*, 1956, pp. 203/4, proposing Guardi as its author. For dating of the Waddesdon *Basin of S. Marco* (and its pendant) see J. Byam Shaw in *Burlington Magazine* (XCVII), 1955, pp. 12 ff.

The Doge's speech in 1780 is given by S. Romanin, *Storia Documentata di Venezia*, 1859, VIII, p. 262. For growth of rationalism, see M. Berengo, *La Società Veneta alla fine del Settecento*, 1956, pp. 243/4. It was Angelo Querini, then safely in Switzerland, who presented the medal to Voltaire: W. Carew Hazlitt, *The Venetian Republic*, 1900 ed., II, p. 317.

Mr. Slade's stay in Venice: W. Buchanan, *Memoirs . . .* , 1824, I, pp. 320 ff.; his catalogue included the picture mentioned (No. 49). The cheapness of G.'s pictures is instanced by a contemporary, see G. Fiocco, *Francesco Guardi*, 1923, p. 8. Strange's letter to Sasso quoted by Mauroner, *Arte Veneta*, 1947, p. 49.

On Migliara (1785–1837) see M. Pittaluga, *Arte Veneta*, 1954, pp. 334 ff.

IV: Genre

Mariette's unfortunate remark about Longhi: 'il devint un autre Watteau' (*Abecedario*, 1856, III, *ad. vocem*) can be accepted only by heavy emphasis upon 'autre'. For some comment on

Pietro Verri, see E. P. Noether, *op. cit.* For his sense of being powerless amid the social conditions of the period in Italy, his own remarks are sufficient, i.e. 'Had I been born in England or in

France, I should be a man like the others . . .' (see further Noether, *op. cit.*, p. 101).

For Longhi as valuer, see M. Brunetti in *Arte Veneta*, 1951, pp. 158 ff. Vertue mentions engravings by Flipart after L.: *Notebooks*, III (*Walpole Society*), p. 154. Orlandi, *op cit.*, 1753 ed., under 'Lunghi' for the 'grossi prezzi' and also for the fact that Agostino Massetti possessed much of L.'s work (a reference yet to be pursued). Maffei's *Sopra il Rinoceronte che si è veduto in Venezia*, 1751, referred to by G. Silvestri, *Un Europeo del Settecento: Scipione Maffei*, 1954, p. 54. At Verona the rhinoceros was drawn by the Tiepolesque Lorenzi 'per Mr. Francesco Seguier francese': D. Zannandreis, *Le Vite dei Pittori . . . Veronesi*, 1891, p. 428.

Gozzi on Longhi: *Gazzetta Veneta*, 1760 (ed. B. Romani), 1943, II, p. 41; *Osservatore Veneto*, 1761, quoted by V. Moschini, *Pietro Longhi*, 1956, pp. 62/63. Gozzi's own witty satiric view of contemporary life is well conveyed in his *Sermoni*.

Grimm's comment quoted by E. Hirschberg, *Die Encyklopädisten und die Französische Oper im 18 Jahrhundert*, 1903, p. 52.

For the fate of P. Felice Cignaroli (who painted the Franciscan *Four Seasons*) see Zannandreis, *op. cit.*, p. 436.

Goldoni's sonnet to Longhi was in the *Raccolta* of poems for the marriage in 1750 of Caterina Contarini and Giovanni Grimani (for latter of whom Longhi's Ca' Rezzonico *Rhinoceros* was painted in the subsequent year); perhaps this is merely a coincidence. Goldoni *Mémoires* (ed. Ortolani), *op. cit.*, p. 263, for what he thought of Chiari's play; for the censorship imposed see Ortolani, *op. cit.*, p. 1106.

For votive pictures connected with guilds and trades at Venice: G. Fogolari in *Dedalo*, 1929, pp. 723 ff.

The life and career of Zompini more than fully discussed in O. Battistella, *Della Vita e delle Opere di Gaetano Gherardo Zompini*, 1930. Amigoni's genre work has remained undiscussed (and unknown?). Wagner's engravings, with English titles, exist. Farinelli's ownership of A.'s genre scenes, in C. Burney, *Present State of Music in France and Italy*, 1773 ed. p. 222.

For Carlo Contarini's speech, see Romanin, *op. cit.*, pp. 244 ff. It was afterwards published, in 1780. The Doge's reply in April 1780 is perhaps most revealing of all statements in the century (already referred to in Chapter III): 'Nel mezzo a tante difficoltà, all' odierna inerzia nostra, al languore, alla lentezza intelletuale e corporea della nazione . . .'; further see Romanin, *op. cit.*, p. 262. By July Contarini was arrested.

For Clemens August's collection, see his sale (after death), Bonn, 14 May *sqq*, 1764. Cochin on Piazzetta, Tiepolo, and nature, cited by A. Fontaine, *Les Doctrines d'Art en France*, 1909, p. 233, note 2.

On Castiglione drawings and paintings collected by Consul Smith, and their popularity in eighteenth-century Venice, see A. Blunt, *The Drawings of Castiglione and Stefano della Bella at Windsor Castle*, 1954, pp. 24 ff.

For Villa Valmarana it might be worth consulting S. Rumor, *I Conti di Valmarana*, 1907 (wherever a copy of this may be). Goethe's comment on the frescoes was not published in the *Italienische Reise*, but see *Goethes Werke* (XI), 1950, p. 586, for what he recorded about his visit. For frescoes still in part remaining at Zianigo see forthcoming article in *The Burlington Magazine* by J. Byam Shaw (who kindly communicated his discovery).

By an unexpected twist of art history, the shift of subject matter for Spanish tapestries was actually caused by Mengs; on this point see for example F. J. Sánchez-Cantón's introduction to the exhibition, *De Tiepolo à Goya*, Bordeaux, 1956, p. xxx.

V: Portrait Painting

Coleridge's comment in *Table Talk*, 1835, I, p. 181.

Goethe on the benevolent appearance of Venetian officials in public: *Italienische Reise, op. cit.*, p. 84.

Crozat's letters to Rosalba among those published by V. Malamani in *Le Gallerie Nazionali Italiane*, 1899, IV, pp. 27 ff. Rosalba's *Diario* published with elaborate annotations in a French ed. by A. Sensier, 1865. Mariette, *Abecedario*, I, p. 330, for Rosalba's incorrectness yet beauty of colour. For, for instance, copies by Mrs. Delany after Rosalba, see letter in *Country Life*, 31 May 1946. Sir Adam Fergusson and Zuccarelli referred to by E. K. Waterhouse, *Painting in Britain 1530–1790*, 1953, p. 175. Crozat's friend M. de Laporte is referred to in a letter published by Malamani, *op. cit.*, p. 132. Crozat on the Polignac sculpture, *loc. cit.*

Nazari's portraits of Tiepolo, Pittoni, Visentini, etc., referred to by Tassi, *Vite de' Pittori . . . Bergamaschi*, 1793, II, p. 92.

The comedy of Mariette and Temanza fully revealed in Mariette's letters in E. Müntz, *Les Archives des Arts*, 1890, pp. 101 ff.

For Amigoni's English portrait work see J. Woodward in *Burlington Magazine* (XCIX), 1957, pp. 21 ff. Burney on the Amigoni portrait: *The Present State of Music in France and Italy*, 1773 ed., p. 220

On a group of 'official' portraits, see T. Pignatti in *Bollettino d'Arte*, 1950, pp. 216 ff. For Joseph Smith's will of 1761, see K. T. Parker, *Canaletto Drawings at Windsor Castle*, 1948, pp. 59 ff., where it is printed in full (spelling modernized in portion quoted in text).

For the three portraits of Francesco Correr by B. Nazari, see Tassi, *op. cit.*, p. 85. Tassi, *loc. cit.*, refers to the equestrian portrait of Schulenburg which was included in the Schulenburg London sale already cited in notes to Chapter III.

Napoleon's reported comment on this portrait by David shows his quick eye for good propaganda: 'Vous m'avez deviné, David: la nuit je travaille au bonheur de mes sujets' etc. Further, see the exhibition catalogue, *David*, Tate Gallery, 1948, p. 26. Fox's request to Reynolds cited in Graves & Cronin, *A History of the Works of Sir Joshua Reynolds, P.R.A.*, 1899, I, p. 332. See E. K. Waterhouse, *Reynolds*, 1941, p. 10, for suggestions (not acceptable) that portraits like No. 3934 in the National Gallery (actually by Alessandro Longhi) influenced Reynolds.

Nogari is usefully reconstructed by H. Honour in *The Connoisseur*, November 1957, pp. 154 ff. Tessin on Nogari: Sirén, *op. cit.*, p. 108. Diderot on La Tour's Rousseau in *Essai sur la Peinture: Œuvres Complètes*, (ed. J. Assézat), 1876, X, p. 483. Goldoni 'rien ne m'interesse . . .' in *Mémoires*, *op. cit.*, p. 81. It was virtually in front of Canova's *Helen* that Byron first met Teresa Guiccioli; see I. Origo, *The Last Attachment*, 1949, p. 37; his comments on the *Helen*, *op. cit.*, p. 494, note 33.

VI: The Presiding Genius: Giambattista Tiepolo

For Eugenia Tiepolo's will, see G. M. Urbani de Gheltof, *Tiepolo e la sua Famiglia*, 1879, pp. 16 ff. For pictures by Canaletto, see Urbani, *op. cit.*, pp. 72/3 (Domenico Tiepolo's will).

Winckelmann's comment on Tiepolo cited by P. Molmenti, *G. B. Tiepolo*, 1909, p. 332. For an English denunciation of Tiepolo's work see for example Bryan's *Dictionary*, 1816 ed., *ad vocem*.

'I pittori presti' comparison, not intended favourably, is in A. Franchi, *La Teorica della Pittura*, 1739, p. 161. See also Reynolds' 12th *Discourse*.

For Lazzarini's *Crossing of the Red Sea* (more than one version) see V. da Canal, *Vita . . .*, 1809, pp. xxxix and liii. Pictures by Lazzarini ex-Smith collection in Strange sale, London, 1789, already cited in Chapter III notes. Strange's comment, under No. 35 of his Catalogue.

Dent's relationship of Scarlatti's characters to the Udine fresco, in his *Alessandro Scarlatti*,

1905, p. 50. Caylus' comment on the *Sacrifice of Iphigenia* (by C. van Loo), *Description d'un tableau . . .*, 1757, p. 22. See also D. Webb's comment on the subject in general, *An Inquiry into the Beauties of Painting . . .*, 1769 ed., p. 147.

Cochin's remarks discussed by J. Seznec in *Journal of the Warburg and Courtauld Institutes*, January/June 1957, p. 108.

The Glasgow project was that of Robert Foulis; *Memorandum* among Foulis papers, Edinburgh University Library. Reynolds on lack of seriousness in Venetian painters, see F. W. Hillis, *The Literary Career of Sir Joshua Reynolds*, 1936, p. 221.

Tessin's note on arriving at Vienna, 'On m'a parlé et fortement recommandé un peintre nommé Tiepoli': Sirén, *op. cit.*, p. 106. Algarotti on the very young Domenico Tiepolo: Posse, *op. cit.*, p. 64.

Diderot on sketches, *Salon* of 1767: *Œuvres Complètes* (ed. J. Assézat), XI, 1876, pp. 245/6. S. Ricci on his own *modello* in a letter to Tassi, Bottari-Ticozzi, *op. cit.*, IV, pp. 93 ff.

Further for the *S. Clement*: M. Levey in *Burlington Magazine* (XCIX), 1957, pp. 256 ff., and A. Morassi in *Arte Veneta*, 1957, pp. 173 ff.

Ruskin on Tiepolo in *St. Mark's Rest* (1st Suppl.), 1887, p. 30.

For the Carmelite scapular and its benefits, see for instance M. A. R. Tuker and H. Malleson, *Handbook to Christian and Ecclesiastical Rome* (Vol. II), 1900, pp. 191/2.

Reynolds' sketch after *Banquet of Cleopatra* is in the British Museum; attention is drawn to it by F. J. B. Watson in *The Connoisseur*, November 1955, p. 214. Comment on the appearance of the Labia ballroom, 'ora abbandonata e squallida', in A. Berti, *Elogio di G. B. Tiepolo: Atti dell'* . . . *Accademia* . . . *in Venezia*, 1856, p. 20. Orlandi, 1753 ed., mentions Mengozzi's work in Palazzo Labia; but not Tiepolo's; perhaps this is significant? Algarotti on the two painters' collaboration in a letter to G. P. Zanotti: Bottari-Ticozzi, *op. cit.*, VII, pp. 397/8. Suggestions that Cleopatra is partly a symbol of Venice made by F. Haskell in *Burlington Magazine* (C), 1958, p. 213. Stothard's *Banquet* for Burley House, still *in situ*. An early post-Renaissance attack on the dangerous beauty of strange women in C. Ripa, *Iconologia*, 1645 ed., p. 464, with special mention of 'gl 'acuti dardi de gli occhi' of Cleopatra.

For Würzburg in full documentary and photographic detail, M. H. von Freeden and C. Lamb, *Das Meisterwerk des G.B.T.*, 1956. Würzburg staircase as Tiepolo's Sistine Chapel: T. Pignatti, *Tiepolo*, 1951, p. 98.

Recently on G. B. Tiepolo at Valmarana, see M. Levey in *Journal of Warburg and Courtauld Institutes*, June/December 1957, pp. 298 ff., but unfortunately not linking the frescoes with Bettinelli (himself asserting the powers of the imagination in an age of 'reason'). For quotations from Bettinelli, his *op. cit.*, pp. 249 ff.

Tiepolo's letter (to Algarotti) of 16 March 1761, with details of his commissions, published by G. Fogolari in *Nuova Antologia*, September 1942, p. 37; for his portrait of Algarotti see M. Precerutti Garberi in *Commentari*, April/June 1958, pp. 120 ff.

For details of Tiepolo's choice in staying in Spain etc. see G. M. Urbani de Gheltof, *Tiepolo in Ispagna*, 1881, pp. 8/9.

The early *S. Francis* (probably a Stigmata) mentioned in Zanetti's ed. of Boschini, *Ricche Minere*, 1733, p. 230. For the Count Seilern *Stigmata* see his catalogue *Italian Paintings and Drawings at 56 Princes Gate*, 1959, (Text) p. 163.

For the disdainful attitude of Voltaire and Diderot (among others) to Watteau, see R. Rey, *Quelques Satellites de Watteau*, 1931, pp. 15 ff. For a 'daub by Gainsborough' contrasted with 'a picture by Sir Joshua', see the letter of Countess Spencer quoted by E. K. Waterhouse, *Reynolds*, 1941, p. 17.

BRIEF BIBLIOGRAPHY

This list omits periodical literature (some references to which are contained in the Chapter notes) and is intended to suggest only further general reading in the subject and books with good plates.

J. Byam Shaw, *The Drawings of Francesco Guardi*. London, 1951.

Nicolas Cochin, *Voyage d'Italie*. Paris, 1758.

G. Delogu, *Pittori Veneti Minori del '700*. Venice, 1929.

J. von Derschau, *Sebastiano Ricci*. Heidelberg, 1922.

Carlo Donzelli, *Pittori Veneziani del Settecento*. Florence, 1957.

Giuseppe Fiocco, *Francesco Guardi*. Florence, 1923.

Giuseppe Fiocco, *Venetian Painting of the Seicento and the Settecento*. London, 1929.

H. Fritzsche, *Bernardo Belotto genannt Canaletto*. Burg b. M., 1936.

Max Goering, *Italienische Malerei des 17. und 18. Jahrhunderts*. Berlin, 1936.

Pietro Gradenigo, *Notizie d'Arte* (ed. L. Livan). Venice, 1942.

D. von Hadeln, *Handzeichnungen von Tiepolo*. Munich, 1927.

I. Haumann, *Das Oberitalienische Landschaftsbild des Settecento*. Strasbourg, 1927.

A. Longhi, *Compendio delle vite de' Pittori Veneziani Istorici*. Venice, 1762.

V. Malamani, *Rosalba Carriera*. Bergamo, 1910.

J.-P. Mariette, *Abecedario*. Paris, 1851–60 (6 vols.).

F. Mauroner, *Luca Carlevarijs*. Padua, 1945 ed.

P. Molmenti, *La Storia di Venezia nella Vita Privata* (vol. III). Bergamo, 1908 ed.

P. Molmenti, *G.B. Tiepolo*. Milan, 1909 (French ed. 1911).

A. Morassi, *Tiepolo*. London, 1955.

V. Moschini, *Guardi*. Milan, 1952.

V. Moschini, *Canaletto*. Milan, 1954.

V. Moschini, *Pietro Longhi*. Milan, 1956.

P. A. Orlandi, *Abecedario* (additions by Guarienti). Venice, 1753 ed.

G. Ortolani, *Voci e Visione del Settecento Veneziano*. Bologna, 1926.

R. Pallucchini, *Gli Affreschi di G.B. e D. Tiepolo alla Villa Valmarana*. Bergamo, 1945.

R. Pallucchini, *Pittura Veneziana del Settecento (Lezioni di Storia dell' Arte)*. Bologna, 1951–2 (2 vols.).

R. Pallucchini, *Piazzetta*. Milan, 1956.

K. T. Parker, *Canaletto Drawings at Windsor Castle*. London, 1948.

T. Pignatti, *Tiepolo*. Milan, 1951.

M. Pittaluga, *Acquafortisti Veneziani del Settecento*. Florence, 1953.

G. Rosa, *Zuccarelli*. Milan, 1945.

E. Sack, *G.B. und D. Tiepolo*. Hamburg, 1910.

G. Simonson, *Francesco Guardi*. London, 1904.

F. J. B. Watson, *Canaletto*. London, 1954 ed.

A. M. Zanetti, *Della pittura veneziana*. Venice, 1771 (2nd ed. 1792).

ACKNOWLEDGEMENTS

The paintings in the Royal Collection are reproduced by gracious permission of Her Majesty the Queen.

The author and publishers are grateful to all private owners who have kindly allowed reproduction of their pictures, particularly to: His Grace the Duke of Buccleuch; Mrs. W. C. C. ten Cate; Lord Cathcart; the Trustees of the Hosmer Estate; George Howard, Esq.; Earl Howe; Mrs. J. Maxwell Macdonald; Count Antoine Seilern; Lord Walpole; also to the Headmaster of Kimbolton School for facilities to photograph fig. 6. Thanks are also due to the authorities of the following public collections for permission to reproduce paintings owned by them: Barber Institute, Birmingham; City Museum and Art Gallery, Birmingham; City Art Gallery, Bristol (bequest of Alfred A. de Pass in memory of Nora de Pass); Wallraf-Richartz-Museum, Cologne; National Gallery of Ireland, Dublin; Kunsthalle, Hamburg; National Gallery, London; National Gallery of Victoria, Melbourne; Alte Pinakothek, Munich; Metropolitan Museum of Art, New York; National Gallery of Art, Washington, D.C.

SOURCES OF PHOTOGRAPHS

Museum photographs: 1, 8, 23, 27, 29, 31, 32, 35, 38, 39, 40, 41, 45, 46, 52, 53, 57, 67, 69, 72, 76, 85, 86, 87, 91
A.F.I., Venice: 83, 84, 88, 107
Alinari, Florence: 2, 13, 14, 47, 65, 78, 80, 81, 82
Anderson, Rome: 37, 105
Fondazione Cini, Venice: 17
Cooper, London: 24, 66
Museo Correr, Venice: 20
Courtauld Institute, London: 26
Ferruzzi, Venice: 103
Fiorentini, Venice: 4, 11, 12, 16, 51, 58, 79, 89
Freeman, London: 6, 33, 90
Gabinetto Fotografico Nazionale, Rome: 49
Manor Studio, London: 68
Foto Marburg: 97
Perotti, Milan: 48
Photo Studio, London: 18, 25, 36, 42, 50, 73, 77
Rijksmuseum, Amsterdam: 21, 44, 75
Rossi, Venice: 3, 10, 19, 28, 61
Gustav Schwarz, Berlin: 15
The Times, London: 43
Wallace Collection, London: 70
Zwicker, Würzburg: 96–99

INDEX OF NAMES

The index contains only names referred to in the text, not in the notes.

Adam, Robert, 51, 69
Addison, Joseph, 53, 71
Albrizzi, Contessa, 161
Albrizzi Giambattista, 38
Algarotti, Francesco, 1, 7, 9 ff., 13, 40, 66, 86, 89, 92, 96, 134, 145, 177, 186, 202
Amigoni, Jacopo, 11, 30 ff., 39, 118, 146 ff., 163; figs. 9, 69
Angelo, Henry, 66
Anne, Queen, 78, 88, 146
Ariosto, Lodovico, 66, 124
Augustus III of Saxony, 145
Austen, Jane, 70, 106

Balestra, Antonio, 39, 42, 73, 106, 109
Baretti, Giuseppe, 7, 66
Batoni, Pompeo, 42
Beccaria, Cesare, 112
Bellini, Gentile, 72
Bellini, Giovanni, 9, 53
Bellotto, Bernardo, 93; fig. 40
Bergeret de Grancourt, 6
Berkeley, George, 2
Bernini, Gian Lorenzo, 140
Bettinelli, Saverio, 198
Bibiena family, 81
Bombelli, Sebastiano, 135 ff., 148, 153; figs. 63, 64
Boschini, Marco, 8
Botticelli, Sandro, 200
Boucher, François, 30, 66, 129, 145, 163
Bourgogne, Duchesse de, 18
Boyne, Lord, 152
Broschi, see Farinelli
Brosses, Charles de, 6
Brown, Rawdon, 78–9
Brühl, Count, 10
Burke, Edmund, 25
Burnet, Bishop, 96
Burney, Charles, 118, 146
Burney, Fanny, 92
Byron, Lord, 92, 161

Campagnola, Domenico, 53
Canal, Vincenzo da, 6, 22, 167
Canaletto, Bernardo, 81
Canaletto, Cristoforo, 81
Canaletto, Giovanni Antonio, 3, 5, 8, 9, 13, 16, 54, 56, 58, 70, 72, 73, 78, 80, 81 ff., 93, 96, 97, 98, 101, 102, 103, 105, 144, 145, 152, 162, 207; figs. 34, 35, 36, 37, 38, 39, 42
Canova, Antonio, 4, 118, 161
Carey, William, 66
Carlevaris, Luca, 73, 75 ff., 82, 92, 93, 96, 98, 152; figs. 31, 32, 33
Carlisle, Lord, 28
Carpaccio, Vittore, 71, 72
Carriera, Giovanna, 140
Carriera, Rosalba, 6, 7, 9, 28, 69, 70, 135, 138 ff., 156, 161, 207; figs. 66, 67, 68
Casanova, Giacomo, 3
Casati, Conte, 173
Cassana, Niccolò, 146
Castellini, Teresa, 146
Castiglione, Gian Battista, 124
Catherine the Great, 46
Caylus, Comte de, 172
Ceruti, Giacomo, 107–8, 122, 128; fig. 48
Chardin, J. B. S., 82
Charles III of Spain, 202
Chatham, Earl of, 10, 66
Chiari, Pietro, 117
Claude Lorrain, 53
Cleeve, Bouchier, 75
Clemens August, Elector, 40, 121, 177
Cochin, Charles N., 6, 12, 18, 22, 39, 40, 122, 146, 173, 204
Cole, Mr., 78
Coleridge, Samuel Taylor, 134, 160
Colloredo, Count, 78
Constable, John, 53–4, 66, 103, 105
Contarini, Carlo, 121
Conti, Stefano, 82
Cornaro, Doge, 148
Corot, J. B. C., 62, 103
Correggio, 19, 138
Correr, Francesco, 148
Costa, Gian Francesco, 96
Courbet, Gustave, 93
Crespi, Giuseppe Maria, 35, 106, 108, 109, 121; fig. 47
Crewe, John, 90
Crozat, Pierre, 7, 140, 145
Cussin, Monsù, 73

David, Jacques Louis, 152
Delacroix, Eugène, 13,
Dent, E. J., 168
Diderot, Denis, 12, 66, 100, 117, 122, 155, 160, 177, 204
Dietrich, C. W. E., 8
Diziani, Antonio, 69
Dolfin, Archbishop, 167
Dryden, John, 13, 188
Dufy, Raoul, 102
Dughet, Gaspard, 53
Dumas, Alexandre, 180
Dürer, Albrecht, 114, 183

Farinelli (Carlo Broschi), 30, 118, 146
Ferdinand de' Medici, 106
Ferdinand VI of Spain, 31
Fergusson, Sir Adam, 144
Feti, Domenico, 42
Filgher, Corrado, 73
Flaubert, Gustave, 160
Fontebasso, Francesco, 46 ff.; fig. 18
Fosse, Charles de la, 22
Fountaine, Sir Andrew, 28
Fox, Charles James, 152
Fragonard, Honoré, 6, 45
Frederick the Great, 1, 10, 11, 152
Frederick of Denmark, 78
Freud, Sigmund, 14

Gainsborough, Thomas, 28, 53, 105, 146, 160, 204; fig. 77
Gautier, Théophile, 92
Geoffrin, Mme, 40
George II, 146, 152
George III, 9, 58, 82
Giaquinto, Corrado, 31
Giordano, Luca, 16 ff.; fig. 2
Giorgione, 8, 73
Giron, Monsù, 73
Goethe, 24, 69, 72, 130, 138, 144
Goldoni, Carlo, 7, 71, 116, 117, 156, 157, 160
Gonzaga family, 135
Goya, Francisco de, 71, 93, 114, 116, 133, 160
Gozzi, Gasparo, 6–7, 60, 115, 116, 154

Gradenigo, Pietro, 6, 97, 115, 116, 152, 153
Gray, Thomas, 58
Greiffenklau, Carl Philipp von, 192 ff.
Greuze, Jean Baptiste, 117, 145
Grimani family, 114
Grimm, Melchior, 116
Guarana, Jacopo, 4, 49 ff.; figs. 19, 20
Guardi, Domenico, 42
Guardi, Francesco, 5, 8, 9, 11, 13, 16, 42 ff., 54, 56, 70, 72, 79, 93, 96 ff., 118 162, 184, 207; figs. 16, 17, 43, 44, 45, 46
Guardi, Giacomo, 103
Guardi, Gian Antonio, 8, 11, 42 ff., 97, 118; figs. 15, 55
Guardi, Nicolò, 42

Hallam, Henry, 92
Haydon, Benjamin, 13
Heintz, Joseph, 73; fig. 30
Helvétius, Claude, 2
Hocheim, Harold von, 192
Hogarth, William, 3, 114, 116
Homer, 124, 198
Hoogh, Pieter de, 111
Huizinga, Jan, 2

Johann Wilhelm, Elector, 28
Johnson, Samuel, 7, 54, 70, 86, 173
Juvarra, Filippo, 58

Kafka, Franz, 4
Kauffmann, Angelica, 92
Kneller, Sir Godfrey, 146

Laclos, Choderlos de, 24
Laporte, de, 145
La Tour, Quentin de, 155
Lazzarini, Gregorio, 6, 163, 164; fig. 78
Leonardo da Vinci, 184
Leopardi, Giacomo, 1
Lessing, Gotthold Ephraim, 13
Liss, Johann, 14, 73
Longhena, Baldassare, 16
Longhi, Alessandro, 4, 6, 7, 70, 114, 118, 153 ff., 164, 207; figs. 74, 75, 76
Longhi, Pietro, 5, 6, 7, 8, 9, 11, 13, 31, 42, 106 ff., 121, 124, 130, 152, 153, 154, 156, 207; figs. 49, 51, 52, 53, 54

Lorenzi, Francesco, 31
Lorenzo da Ponte, 13
Loth, Carl, 14, 36, 73; fig. 1
Louis XIV, 18, 160
Louis XV, 140, 144

McSwiny, Owen, 58, 82
Maffei, Francesco, 138; fig. 65
Maffei, Scipione, 4, 114
Magnasco, Alessandro, 54, 60, 68
Manchester, Earl of, 25, 26, 78, 140
Manet, Édouard, 112
Mantegna, Andrea, 9
Marieschi, Michiel, 54, 93; fig. 41
Mariette, Jean-Pierre, 5, 7, 10, 28, 112, 140, 144, 146
Mengozzi-Colonna, Agostino, 51
Mengozzi-Colonna, Girolamo, 176, 184 ff.
Mengs, Anton Raphael, 25, 31, 42, 163, 202; fig. 105
Metastasio, Pietro, 146, 163
Michelangelo, 39
Migliara, Giovanni, 105
Molinari, Antonio, 35
Montagu, Lady Mary Wortley, 1
Montesquieu, 1
Moore, Dr, 72
Moretti, Giuseppe, 92
Moschini, Gian Antonio, 81
Mozart, Wolfgang Amadeus, 129, 163, 207
Murger, Henri, 164
Murillo, 108
Murray, John, 9

Napoleon, 1, 105, 152, 160
Nazari, Bartolomeo, 75, 145, 148 ff.; fig. 70
Nazari, Nazario, 148, 152; fig. 72
Nerval, Gérard de, 144
Neumann, Balthasar, 192, 193
Newton, Sir Isaac, 10
Nogari, Giuseppe, 153
Northcote, James, 2

Ovio, Paolo, 78

Panini, Gian Paolo, 56
Parini, Giuseppe, 112

Passeri, Niccolò, 25
Pellegrini, Giovanni Antonio, 7, 25 ff., 31, 38, 39, 54, 78, 140, 163, 176; figs. 6, 7, 8, 85
Piazzetta, Giambattista, 11, 14, 32 ff., 40, 58, 80, 106, 108, 109, 121 ff., 124, 145, 164, 177, 198; figs. 10, 12, 13, 57
Picasso, Pablo, 39, 122
Piero della Francesca, 96
Piozzi, see Thrale
Piranesi, Giambattista, 42
Pisani family, 114, 118, 202
Pisani, Alvise, 78
Pisani, Podestà, 138
Pitt, see Chatham
Pittoni, Francesco, 39
Pittoni, Giambattista, 11, 39 ff., 48, 58, 145, 177; fig. 14
Pliny, 184, 188
Plutarch, 184
Polignac, Cardinal de, 145
Ponte, Lorenzo da, 3
Pope, Alexander, 88
Poussin, Nicolas, 25, 39
Proust, Marcel, 184

Racine, Jean, 176
Ramelli, Felice, 140
Ramsay, Allan, 134
Redgrave, Samuel and Richard, 66–7
Rembrandt, 9, 14, 135, 153, 182
Renoir, 112, 140
Reynolds, Sir Joshua, 12, 134, 152, 153, 163, 174, 184; fig. 73
Ricci, Marco, 8, 9, 22, 25–6, 39, 54 ff., 68, 78, 82, 93, 98; figs. 21, 22, 23, 24
Ricci, Sebastiano, 7, 8, 9, 11, 19 ff., 27, 28, 30, 31, 32, 36, 39, 42, 45, 46, 48, 49, 54, 58, 82, 145, 164, 168, 174, 177; figs. 3, 4, 5, 11, 23
Richard, Abbé, 3
Richardson, Samuel, 24, 92
Richmond, Duke of, 58
Richter, Gustave, 73
Rilke, Rainer Maria, 122
Rosa, Salvator, 53, 54, 60, 68, 75
Rosalba, see Carriera
Rose, W. Stewart, 92

Rotari, Pietro, 42
Rousseau, Jean-Jacques, 2, 155, 160
Rubens, P. P., 10, 135
Ruskin, John, 6, 70, 88, 96, 180

Sagredo family, 114
Sand, George, 180
Sasso, Gian Maria, 7, 8, 105
Scarlatti, Alessandro, 26, 168
Schulenburg, Marshal, 75, 93, 122, 152
Sebastiano del Piombo, 73
Shaw, George Bernard, 2
Shelley, Percy Bysshe, 88
Simonson, George, 105
Slade, Thomas Moore, 103
Smith, Joseph, 7, 9, 58, 62, 82, 83, 85, 140, 141, 145, 148, 164
Solimena, Francesco, 134
Stanislas Poniatowski, 93
Steele, Richard, 66
Stothard, Thomas, 188
Strange, John, 7, 8, 75, 96, 105, 164
Styles, Mr, 31

Tasso, Torquato, 124
Temanza, Tommaso, 146
Teniers, David, 122, 204
Tessin, Count, 32, 40, 153
Thornhill, Sir James, 20, 31
Thrale, Mrs, 7, 92
Tickell, Thomas, 60
Tiepolo, Domenico, the elder, 164

Tiepolo, Eugenia, 162
Tiepolo, Giambattista, 1, 2, 5, 6, 8, 9, 10, 11, 13, 16, 18, 19, 22, 28, 30, 31, 34, 36, 39, 40, 46, 48, 49, 51, 52, 67, 80, 96, 101, 115, 116, 118, 121, 122, 124, 130, 145, 152, 162 ff.; figs. 79–84, 86–104, 106, 107, 115
Tiepolo, Giovanni Domenico, 124 ff., 176, 177, 191, 196 f., 201, 202, 204, 207; figs. 58–62
Tiepolo, Lorenzo, 191, 202, 204
Tintoretto, Jacopo, 6, 14, 18, 19, 46, 80, 97, 135, 179
Tintoretto, Domenico, 135, 138
Titian, 6, 8, 10, 14, 18, 19, 53, 54, 97, 134, 135, 163, 179
Tron, Andrea, 152
Troost, Cornelis, 110–11, 112; fig. 50
Turner, J. M. W., 88, 103

Uberti, Pietro, 148, 152; fig. 71
Udny, John, 148

Valéry, Paul, 18
Vanbrugh, John, 26, 28
Vanvitelli, *see* Wittel
Valmarana, Gaetano, 124
Vasari, Giorgio, 163
Velazquez, Diego, 135
Vermeer, Johannes, 9, 111
Veronese, Paolo, 6, 8, 10, 14, 18, 19, 22, 25, 27, 36, 51, 135, 164, 167, 174, 176, 180, 200

Verri, Pietro, 112
Vertue, George, 114
Vien, Joseph-Marie, 40
Villon, François, 73
Virgil, 124
Visentini, Antonio, 62, 85, 86, fig. 25
Voltaire, 2, 3, 102, 160, 204

Wagner, Giuseppe, 118
Walpole, Horace, 9, 32, 144
Watteau, Antoine, 7, 68, 112, 122, 138, 204
Wilde, Oscar, 88
Wilson, Richard, 60, 62, 66, 134
Winckelmann, Johann Joachim, 25, 163, 174, 198
Wittel, Gaspar van, 73 ff.
Wren, Sir Christopher, 28
Wyck, Jan, 86

Zais, Giuseppe, 67 ff., 93; figs. 28, 29
Zanetti, Anton Maria the elder, 7, 8, 9, 57, 140
Zanetti, Anton Maria the younger, 8–9, 44, 54, 57, 60, 82, 118
Zanetti, Girolamo, 56
Zenobio family, 78
Zola, Emile, 106
Zompini, Gaetano, 118 ff.; fig. 56
Zuccarelli, Francesco, 9, 11, 53, 56, 60 ff., 68, 69, 70, 86, 144; figs. 25, 26, 27